Stalingrad

Perry Pierik & Peter Steeman

STALINGRAD

The Battle and the Air Bridge to Death

ASPEKT PUBLISHERS

STALINGRAD

© 2023 ASPEKT Publishers
© Introduction Perry Pierik (red.)

Amersfoortsestraat 27, 3769 AD Soesterberg, The Netherlands info@uitgeverijaspekt.nl - http://www.uitgeverijaspekt.nl

Translation: Isabel Oomen
Editor: Aspekt Graphics

ISBN: 9789464870534
NUR: 680

All rights reserved. No part of this publication may be reproduced, stored in a retrieval system or transmitted in any form or by any means, electronic, mechanical, photocopying, recording or otherwise, without the prior permission of the publisher.

Foreword

With the launch of the operation under the code name '*Fall Blau*', the new German summer offensive in Russia in 1942, the dramatic chapter of Stalingrad, began. The city on the Volga was initially not even mentioned in the German plans. Nevertheless, the operations developed in such a way that a titanic battle finally took place, which was partly decisive for the further course of World War II. In this book, we dwell above all on the air bridge to the city. The German 6th Army, after being surrounded by the Red Army, had become dependent on logistical support from outside and only an air bridge could help.

Air Force commander Hermann Göring guaranteed the supply of sufficient goods, including large quantities of ammunition, but it immediately became clear that this was not possible. The troops at Stalingrad slowly died off. Even the transport of wounded was flawed and eventually became impossible. Besides the battle over the city, there is also extensive coverage of the prelude to Stalingrad, during which a number of interesting things happened that are not so widely known. For instance, the 1942 summer offensive did not start from the German side, but from the Russian side. Today, we would call that a *pre-emptive strike*. In the front sector near Kharkov, the Red Army tried to break through to the southwest. Through a hastily constructed counterattack, operation '*Fridericus*', the attack was parried and the Soviets were dealt a heavy blow. Along other fronts too, the Stalingrad preliminaries were extremely bloody, such as at Sebastopol, Kerch, Woronesch and at Kalatsch, just before Stalingrad. In many ways, this final showdown was a turning point. It was the last classic German encirclement battle in which the Red Army became enclosed with large units.

Stalingrad was a great human tragedy on both sides. Those who delve into the battle and the human suffering cannot help but conclude that this suffering was universal. Stalingrad became the grave for thousands of conscript militia who often, regardless of any ideological concept, simply fought for their own survival. In addition, the city's civilian population suffered enormously, and horrific stories are known about the fate of Russian and German prisoners of war. All the same, Stalingrad did mark the turning point in what historians have increasingly come to see as an 'extermination campaign'. Operation '*Barbarossa*', the German attack on the Soviet Union, was dominated by Nazi ideology from the outset. Communist commissars, local administrators, partisans and Jews were hunted down from the first days, and so- called '*Einsatzgruppen*' (SD murder squads) operated right behind the front with unprecedented terror.

This book focuses on the German military and political decision-making that led to the Stalingrad debacle; and furthermore the air bridge that followed the military *fiasco* on Volga and Don. Through text, maps specially produced for this book, and gripping photographs, the reader is transported to the famous battle on the Eastern Front. This book makes clear that Stalingrad was not an isolated event, but part of an endless series of bloody battles. Furthermore, it shows how generals and the political leadership of Nazi Germany gradually alienated themselves from reality and provided orders from *Führer headquarters* to an army that was sinking in cold, hunger, despair and death.

The authors

'Fall Blau'

Paulus (commander 6th Army)*: Ich verstehe nicht, entweder habe ich das Kommandieren verlernt - oder Gott ist auf ihrer Seite!*

Schmidt: *Herr Generaloberst, Gott ist immer auf der Seite der starken Bataillone.*

(Nikolaj Wirta in *Die Stalingrader Schlacht*)

After the failed 1941 summer offensive, 'Operation *Barbarossa*', the German army faced a major task in the summer of 1942. With the weather once again favourable for offensive operations, Nazi Germany wanted to regain the initiative. This time, the battle would have Hitler's stamp even more than before. The gaze turned southwards, towards the oil fields of the Caucasus and the military operations between the Donets and Don rivers, which were to pave the way for the offensive towards the black gold of Baku and Grozny. Hitler attached significant geopolitical, military and economic value to oil. The well-known German tank specialist Heinz Guderian even believed that for Hitler, oil was 'written in capital letters'. Not only in the summer of 1942, but right up to the end of the war, Hitler would fight for the Third Reich's oil reserves; be it the Romanian fields near Ploesti, the Hungarian fields near Nagykanisza or the small fields of Austrian Zisterdorf. Stalingrad initially played hardly any role in the preparatory plans of the German supreme command. The city on the Volga, named after Stalin, would eventually surface on a wave of destruction.

Hitler's decision to launch an offensive on the southern front stemmed from realism as well. The offensive strength of the German army was reduced to the point where no full-scale attack was possible by April 1942. The German army numbered more than 8.5 million soldiers in April 1942, of which more than 2.6

million were in the east. With this, a significant weakening (dead, wounded, missing) had occurred since the start of the attack against the Soviet Union on 22 June 1941. Although the eastern front had received 1 million reinforcements since the start of the hostilities, there was a shortfall of 625,000 men which Nazi Germany could not fill. Millions of German soldiers were stationed on other fronts, more than half a million in France alone, as Berlin constantly feared invasion. Moreover, the battle in Africa cost troops. When the snow of the long Russian winter melted, the German army in the east was in poor shape, to say the least. Only eight of the 162 infantry divisions in Russia (status 30.03.1942) were fully deployable, and three divisions could be after a short rest. Of the remaining 151, 47 divisions were considered capable of carrying out limited attacks, the rest of the infantry was only suitable for defensive tasks in which it had to be taken into account that 29 divisions could only carry out limited defensive tasks and 2 divisions actually had some combat value only on paper. In the panzer troops, the situation was dramatic as well. At the end of March, the 16 armoured divisions (*Pz.Div.*) in Russia had a tank stock which could just fill one division to pre-war standards, namely 140 deployable tanks. Of course, not all defective tanks were gone, and much could be absorbed by maintenance and repair. Nevertheless, the German army in the summer of 1942 was weaker than in 1941. Hitler therefore had to make choices, and that choice became the southern front: operation '*Siegfried*', which would later go down in history as Plan (*Fall*) '*Blau*', later changed again to '*Braunschweig*', or colloquially: the battle of Stalingrad.

That Hitler was serious about *Fall Blau* was evident on 13 April 1942. He paid a personal visit to another very important front sector: the Army Group North (*Heeresgruppe Nord*) which was on the Wolchov River and had drawn a deadly ring of encirclement around Leningrad. The northern front section had several important military and geopolitical hang-ups, not least the alliance with the Finns for which Hitler held admiration. He would make time during the 1942 summer offensive to visit the Finnish commander-in-chief Mannerheim personally on his birthday. There were 'important tasks' in the south, Hitler believed; the Caucasus and oil. Army reinforcements would go to that front sector. Internally at the OKW, the army's supreme command, Hitler let it be known that he wanted only the best officers in the south.

Führer-Weisung no. 41

The attack laid down in '*Führer-Weisung nr. 41*', provided for three operations: from north to south, from the area around the city of Orel, the 2nd Army and the 4th Pz.Army (Von Weichs, and Hoth) would advance towards the city of Woronesch and then turn south, following the river Don. Next, the 6th Army (Paulus) would push eastward from the area around the city of Kharkov to join the 4th Pz.Army in encircling the Russian forces west of the Don. This '*Kessel*' (encirclement) was to occur in the Nowo- Oskol area. The southernmost was where the 17th Army (Ruoff) together with parts of the 1st Pz.Army (von Kleist) came into action. These opereated from the Taganrog-Rostov area and attacked along the lower Don River. Subsequent operations further into the Caucasus were summarised in *Weisung No 45*, on 23 July 1942.

Part of *Weisung No 41, 'Fall Blau'* also included the capture of Crimea. The German 11th Army (Von Manstein) had been active on the peninsula since the autumn of 1941. The city of Sebastopol was strongly fortified and therefore a powerful *bastion* of the Red Army. The Russians had skillfully dug in, which make things difficult for the 11th Army. Other parts of Crimea were more difficult for the Russians to defend. The *Wehrmacht* captured the town of Kerch and the peninsula of the same name on 17 November 1941, which meant they now stood at the Strait of Asov and the Black Sea.

Kerch - Sebastopol

However, the German troops in Crimea were facing the same dilemma as the other units of *Heeresgruppe Süd*, as we shall see later. There were too few troops to exert sufficient pressure everywhere at the right time. As Von Manstein concentrated more on the Sebastopol fortress, things became unsettled again on the eastern flank near Kerch. The Russian Black Sea fleet landed new units there. The German army had to respond again, out of necessity. Units had to rejoin eastward from the Sebastopol front to face the new danger. Although Stalin's plans were ambitious, the Russians failed to recapture Crimea. Around April 1942, Von Manstein was able to regain the initiative and once again increased the pressure on Sebastopol.

On 8 May 1942, Operation '*Trappenjagd*' started, in which the peninsular island of Kerch was once again captured from the Red Army. Between 8 and 13 May, the heaviest fighting raged around the so-called '*Tatarenwall*', twenty kilometres west of Kerch.

The failed Sebastopol attempt had become a disaster for the Russian intervention force, which consisted of 26 units of about divisional strength from the 44th, 47th and 51st Armies. Kerch became the bloody Russian version of Dunkirk: a death trap. The Red Army had been pushed back into a front sector only 18 kilometres wide with water on both sides of the peninsula. Divisions were on top of each other. One clung to defensive lines that were right on the German advance route; the Parpacht Nasyr - and Sultanovka - lines that were under frontal attack by Von Manstein's German 11th Army. Lacking room to manoeuvre, the Russian positions had to be broken one by one. The deployment of the *Luftwaffe* was therefore of great importance.

The deployment of the *Luftwaffe* in Crimea was threefold. First, there were the operations against Sebastopol, second, against Red Army units on Kerch and finally, cutting off the water-road between Kerch and the Soviet hinterland. Especially the ports of Kerch, Kamish-Burun and Novorossiisk were important targets here for *Luftflotte 4* (*Generaloberst* Löhr) an *Flieger Corps VIII* (*Generaloberst* Wolfram von Richthofen).

For Hitler, repelling the Russian offensive on Kerch and eliminating Sebastopol were a basic prerequisite for success in the south. Wolfram von Richthofen was specifically recalled from his holiday for it. Von Richthofen was known as a troublesome and rough fighter, but one of the most talented tacticians within the *Luftwaffe*. Especially direct support of ground troops with the *Junkers 87* (*Stukas*) was part of his specialty. The *Stukas* (*Sturzkampfflugzeug*) were fragile dive-bombers that had had a tough time against British fighters in the '*Battle of Britain*'. However, here in the Crimea where the Germans had air superiority, they were great for deployment and were particularly lethal weapons against the packed Russian divisions. From his *Storch reconnaissance aircraft,* Von Richthofen was constantly on the move, tracking both his air units and German ground forces. There was a once-in-a-lifetime opportunity to destroy three Russian armies right at the beginning of the 1942 summer field campaign. The Red air force - numerically similar in the Crimean region but tactically less capable - could not stop him. Heavy bombers were deployed from *Nikolayev* and *Kherson* airfields in Ukraine, while German fighters and *Stukas* operated from *Saki*, *Simferopol* and *Sarabus*, closer to the front. *Grammatikovo* airfield was about 40 kilometres from the front. Successes did not fail to materialise. On 8 May 1942, Von Richthofen spoke of a '*Riesen-Feuerzauber*' (giant magic fire - a fireworks display) over the Kerch, when he saw the

2,100 *operations* of the *Luftwaffe* described. He noted that the Russian front was on the verge of collapse. 'Lots of dead Russians, guns, several thousand completely demoralised prisoners,' he wrote in his diary. The next day, the chase continued unabated with 1,700 sorties in which 1,500 tonnes of bombs were dropped on the crowded troops, resulting in carnage. That day, Von Richthofen concluded in his diary: 'The battle of Kerch has been won, though not yet concluded!'

The Red air force did what it could, but paid a heavy price in the defence of Kerch. Von Richthofen reported the loss of 82 Russian aircraft on 8 May and 42 machines on 9 May. German losses were relatively modest: ten flying machines on the 8th and two on the 9th. 'Weather permitting, no Russian will leave Crimea alive,' he noted with satisfaction. 'Highest attainable blood and materiel loss,' Von Richthofen wrote on 11 May, noting that the German troops, as well as the Romanians, on the ground were getting a better and better grip on the Russian armies. 'All the equipment is left lying around, everyone is trying to save their live'.

The bridge at Woronesch, 1942

Korpsgruppe Blümm
Ia Nr. 71/42 g.Kdos.

Gr.Gef.Std., den 4.8.1942.

30 Ausfertigungen.
5. Ausfertigung.

Korpsgruppenbefehl
für das "Unternehmen Eingemeindung".

1.) Feindgliederung gegenüber Korpsgruppe Blümm hat sich bisher nicht wesentlich geändert. Trotz vermehrter fdl. Schanztätigkeit ist nicht damit zu rechnen, daß der Feind seine Angriffsabsichten auf den Brückenkopf Woronesh aufgegeben hat. Die derzeitige ruhige Kampflage ist wohl auf die hohen blutigen Verluste zurückzuführen, die der Feind bei seinen bisherigen Angriffen auf den Brückenkopf erlitten hat.

Es ist damit zu rechnen, daß der Feind nach Auffüllung und Neugliederung seiner Verbände erneut zum Angriff besonders an der Süd- und Nordfront des Brückenkopfes antreten wird. Gegenüber eigenen Angriffen wird sich der Russe auf Grund der zuletzt bekanntgewordenen Befehle Stalin's zäh in seinen Stellungen verteidigen.

2.) Korpsgruppe Blümm hat durch Angriff die Nordfront des Brückenkopfes so weit vorzuverlegen, daß der Besitz der Stadt für dauernd sichergestellt ist.

Der Angriff ist unter dem Decknamen "Unternehmen Eingemeindung" so vorzubereiten, daß er ab 8.8.42 auf besonderen Befehl durchgeführt werden kann.

8.8.42 = X - Tag.

Der Befehl zum Angriff wird zeitgerecht übermittelt und ausgelöst durch das Stichwort: "Unternehmen Eingemeindung X - Tag, 6.00 Uhr" oder "X + ... Tag, ... Uhr usw.".

Durch vermehrtes auffälliges Schanzen ist beim Feind der Eindruck zu erwecken, daß keine Angriffshandlungen von unserer Seite beabsichtigt sind.

Der Korpsgruppe Blümm werden für den Angriff ab 5.8.42 0.00 Uhr neu unterstellt und zugeführt:

    75. Inf.Div.
    Artl.Kdeur.139
    Artl.Abt.709 (10 cm)
    III./A.R.111 (s.F.H.)
    II./A.R.109 (Mrs.)
    Sturmgesch.Abt.190
    Pz.Jäg.Abt.560 (mot.Z.).

3.) Trennungslinien der Korpsgruppe Blümm zu den Nachbarn bleiben unverändert.

– 2 –

Commander of the bridges: Woronesch, corps order

Korpsgruppe Blümm
Ia Nr. 609/42 geh.

K.Gr.Gef.Std., den 30.N(1942.

Korpsgruppenbefehl Nr.9

1.) Feind setzte in den letzten Tagen seine Angriffe gegen den Brückenkopf Woronesh nur mit Teilvorstößen fort, stellt aber weitere Kräfte besonders gegenüber dem Südabschnitt bereit.
Es ist zu erwarten, daß der Feind an seiner Absicht, Woronesh wieder zu gewinnen, unverändert festhält und sehr bald erneut zum Angriff gegen den Brückenkopf Woronesh antritt.

2.) Aufgabe der Korpsgruppe Blümm bleibt unverändert die Verteidigung des Brückenkopfes Woronesh. Brückenschläge über den Woronesh sind durch 323.Div. mit allen Mitteln zu verhindern, wenn nötig, durch Vorziehen einzelner Geschütze in offene Feuerstellung.

3.) Trennungslinien:
zur kgl. ung.Armee:
Bahn Lgoff – Ryschkowo (ung.) – Tim Süd – Gorschetschnoje Süd – Mündung des Woronesh in den Don – Panino Nord – Mutschka Süd.
zum VII.A.K.:
Bhf. Nishnedewizk (Blümm) – Nishne Weduga (Blümm) – Titowka (VII) – Studenyi (Blümm) – Jamnaja (VII) – Bhf. Grafskaja (Blümm).
Rückwärtige Grenze des Gefechtsgebietes:
Nishnedewizi (einschl.) – Kastornoje (ausschl.).

4.) Im Gebiet der Korpsgruppe Blümm sind zur Verfg. der Armee untergebracht:
75.Inf.Div. im Raum Stempelja – Wolchonskoj – Turowo – Lagowskaja – Nishnedewizi – W.Nikolskoje.
1.SS-Inf.Brig.: um Nishne – Weduga.

5.) Durch Aufklärung und Stoßtruppunternehmen muß ständig Klarheit über Stärke und Gliederung des gegenüberliegenden Feindes aufrecht erhalten bleiben.
Belassen oder erneutes Vorschieben von Gefechtsvorposten ist an allen Stellen der Front anzustreben.

6.) Der Ausbau des Hauptkampffeldes ist mit allem Nachdruck weiterzutreiben. Möglichste Panzersicherheit hat überall den Vorrang. Auf gründlichste Zerstörung der vor der HKL liegenden Häuser und Keller wird nochmals hingewiesen. Das Schußfeld ist freizumachen.
Einbau von innerhalb der eigenen Linien abgeschossenen Feindpanzern als Pak oder B-Stelle im Hauptkampffeld kann in Frage kommen.
Die derzeitigen hohen Ausfälle an Pferden und Fahrzeugen lediglich durch Splitterwirkung veranlassen mich, erneut darauf hinzuweisen, daß Pferde und Fahrzeuge gegen Splitterwirkung einzugraben sind.

– 2 –

Instruction about the defense of Woronesch

Signposts placed at a rifle at Woronesch

Buried tank at Woronesch

Street view Woronesch. For months, there would be an exhaustive and hopeless battle here

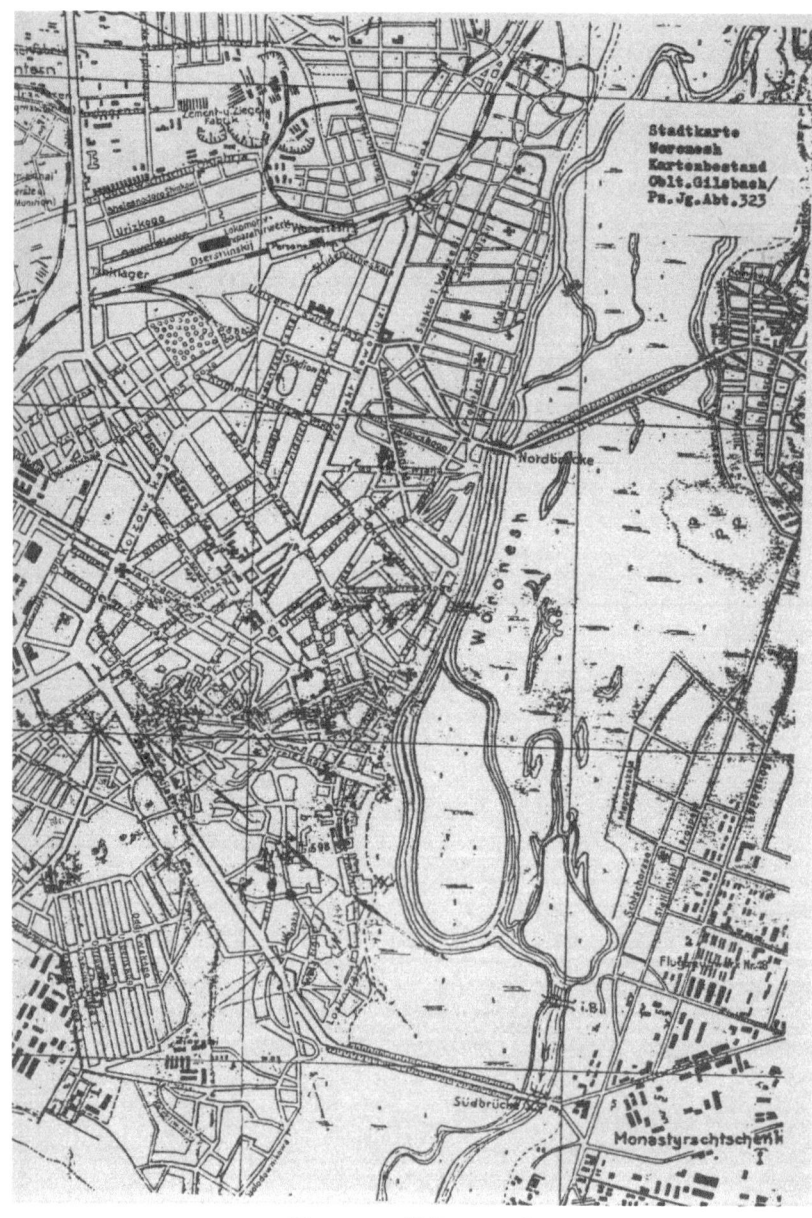

City map of Woronesch

German soldier in Woronesch

Woronesch, disabled Soviet tank, July 1942

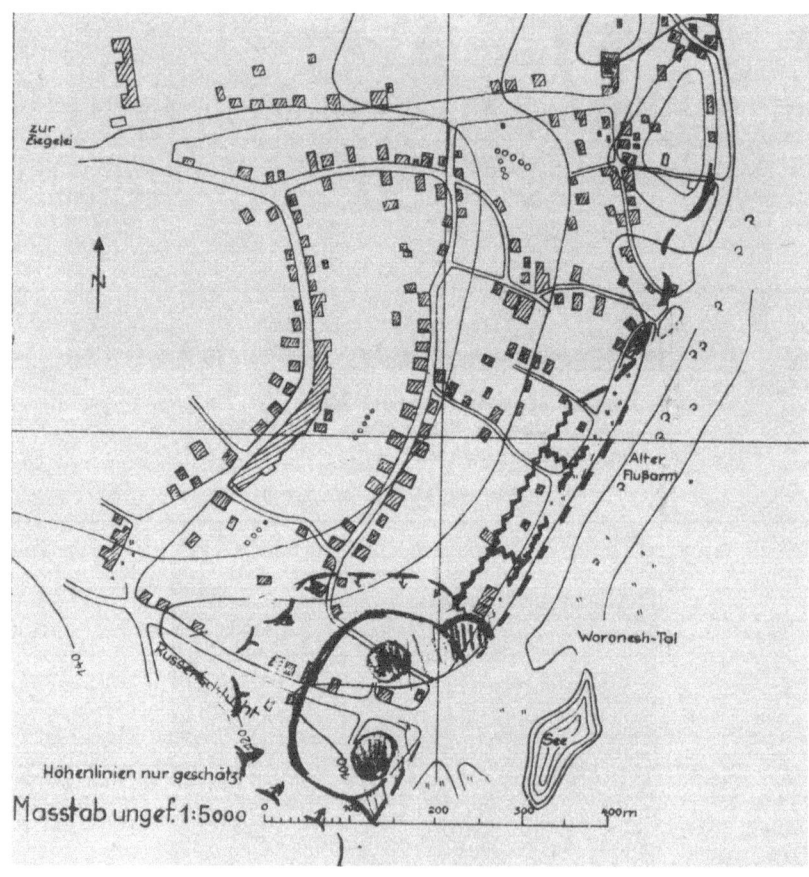

Woronesch

Red Square, Woronesch centre, 1942

Party house on the Red Square, Woronesch 1942

*Military discussion at Hitler's Führer Headquarters, from left to right:
Von Manstein, Ruoff, Hitler, Zeitzler en Von Kleist*

General List (Heeresgruppe A) and Generaloberst Von Kleist (1. Pz. leger)

Kharkov - Soviets Attack First

Nothing seemed to stand in the way of the destruction of the total Russian army force, when suddenly there was a hitch in *Fall Blau*. Even before the German offensive against Woronesch and the in-turn between Don and Donets could take place, the Russians opened a '*pre-emptive*' offensive in the front sector near Kharkov.

The OKW diary already reported extensive Red Army troop movements on 4 May, 6 May and 11 May 1942, and the next day the Russian counterattack east and south of Kharkov, against the German 6th Army (Paulus), was a fact. That this would have consequences for the battle for Kerch was immediately clear. '*Bei Charkow scheinbar riesige Schweinerei*', Von Richthofen noted.

Kharkov was an important supply city, a road hub and the fifth largest city in the Soviet Union. The 6th Army had conquered the prestigious place on 24 October 1941, which had effectively marked the end of the 1941 summer conquest, the birth year of '*Barbarossa*'. With their actions against Kerch and now again against Kharkov, or more precisely from the territory north of Kharkov and south of the city, around Ishum, it was in fact the Soviets who took the initiative. Here, the Russians exploited the front arc that stabbed westward into the German flesh. The German supreme command, after the arduous winter fighting in this front section, had already planned, working together through the 1st Armoured Army and the 17th Army, to deal with this breakthrough in a concentric (encirclement) attack (operation '*Fridericus*'). However, the Soviets, led by Semyon K. Timoshenko, were ahead of the Germans. Timoshenko's wish-list, with five armies and very many tanks, included the city of Kharkov and a further push to Dniepropetrowsk and Saporoschje, famous for its dam. Timoshenko, with his characteristic bald skull, was steeled in battle: partisan war in Crimea in 1918, cavalry commander under Budjonny, the Finnish and Polish campaigns, and trained at the *Frunze* and *Lenin* academies.

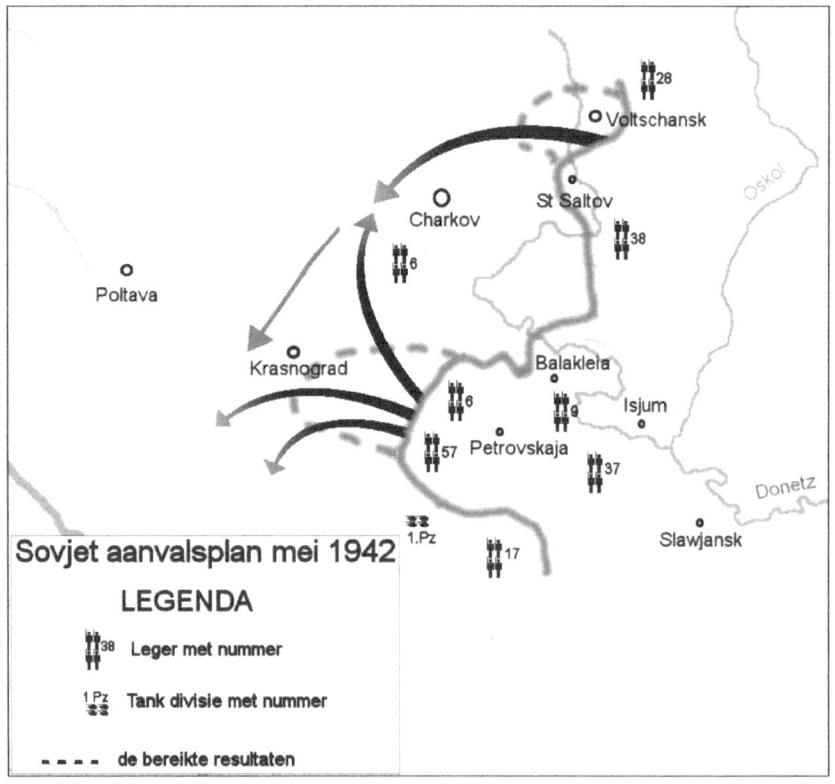

Soviet plan of attack, May 1942

Legend
- Army with number
- Tank division with number
- The achieved goals

Operation Fridericus - the German Response to the Kharkov Offensive

The outcome of this battle would determine '*Fall Blau*'. From north to south, between Woltschansk north of Kharkov, and Slavyansk (Sslavyansk) south of Kharkov, the 28th, 38th, 6th, 57th and 9th Russian Armies attacked. The southern thrust from the Ishum river basin was unstoppable. A breakthrough towards Krasnograd was a fact. Hitler recognised the danger, but also wanted to push '*Fridericus*' through. Reinforcements were needed immediately, and at flying speed, *Luftwaffe* units were stripped from the Crimea and the front at Kerch. Von Richthofen gritted his teeth. Nevertheless, Kretsch was a successful battle of annihilation for the Germans. The town of the same name was recaptured on 16 May 1942 by the German 170th Infantry Division and *Regiment 213*.

At the same time, the situation around Kharkov was 'tense', as noted in the OKW's diary. Hitler wanted to deploy '*Fridericus*' as a countermeasure, but the German generals pointed out that absorbing Tymoshenko's attack demanded all forces. Around the same day, the Russian attack thrust to a climax. German infantry and tank units that were quickly dispersed managed to slow down the Soviet force while strong air units reinforced the front. Red Army tank losses began to mount rapidly. On 16 May, the OKW reported that Tymoshenko's forces had lost their 179th tank since the beginning of the offensive. This was the go-ahead to launch '*Fridericus*' southern line of attack ('*Süd*'), i.e. a 'half' version of the original plan, the next day.

German commander Von Bock, on the other hand, was not yet sure of his case and tried to get units from '*Fall Blau*' for his counterattacks. Hitler, however, stuck to the old plan. The next day, Von Kleist's breakthrough with armoured units took place in Tymoshenko's exit area around the Ishum. The Russians were taken completely by surprise by '*Fridericus*'. Meanwhile, the 6th Army caught blow after blow and destroyed the Red Army's 296th tank. These results notwithstanding, Red Army cavalrymen penetrated Krasnograd. '*Fridericus*' came not a day too soon. The positions near Kharkov held. Attacks and counterattacks alternated here. On 19 May, Hitler himself compared the showdown to the important battle of Tannenberg where Von Hindenburg and Ludendorff prevented the Tsarist army from invading East Prussia in 1914. Again, they had to grit their teeth and persevere. *Generaloberst* Halder of the OKW already foresaw that '*Fridericus*' would give air and it eventually did.

19 May was a sunny day and units of the 16th Pz.Division, as well as other German units were cutting deeper and deeper into Timoshenko's army hinterland. The division had been railroaded to the front. In order not to lose the surprise effect, the division had been transported company-wise. Before the counterattack, General Hube had encouraged the men on the large meadow near Tschaikino: 'The road to mother, bride, wife or children runs only by a diversion to the east'.

Via Stalino - Yassinowataya - Artemowsk, the unit was directed to the front. There were reasonable tarmac roads in the area and the division headed towards the threatened sector with utmost speed. At Slavyansk, the troops assembled. The men of the 384th Inf.Div., who were in the area, looked up in amazement when suddenly so many tanks gathered. 'It looked like an ant- heap in the city,' wrote Wolfgang Werthen, author of the war history of the 16th Pz.Div. Tymoshenko suspected nothing yet. In the previous days, Slawjansk had been regularly shelled by Soviet artillery, but now the guns were silent. At 03.05, German artillery opened fire, the 16th Pz.Division as an part of the XXXXIV Army Corps (*Gruppe 'Hube'*) opened the surprise attack, supported by units of the 97th, 384th and 68th Inf. Division. The deeply built-up Soviet winter positions were trampled underfoot. In *unerhörtem Schwung*, Werthen wrote. Russian units

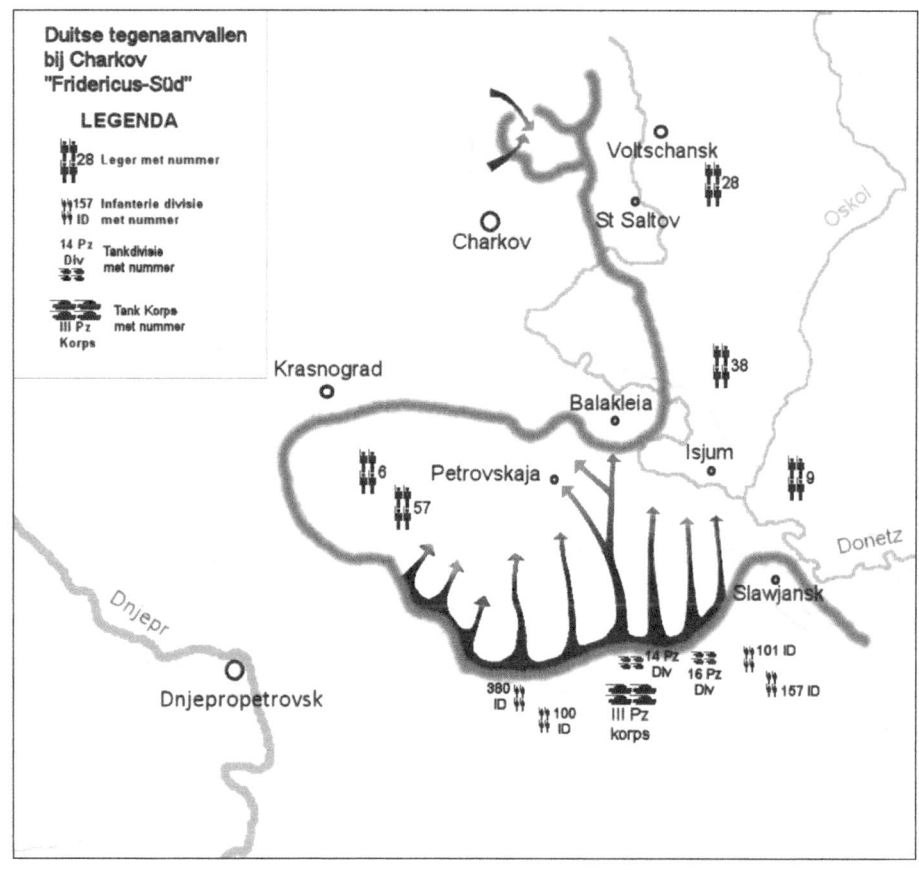

German counter attacks at Charkov 'Fridericus-Süd'

Legend
- Army with number
- Infantry division with number
- Tank division with number
- Tank corps with number

fought bravely as ever, but battalions were isolated in their positions and rolled up in hand-to-hand combat by the battle group *Witzleben* and battalion *Muews*. The Russians were taken completely by surprise. At Dubrowka, Timosjenko still tried to recover. Regiments of field infantry banded together, but were dispersed by the tanks and artillery. The retreat route to Ishum was now barred to the Russians. By the next day, the OKW was already bent over the maps of '*Fall Blau*' and delving into the obstacles that awaited them there: the 'settlement cities' in the area: Rostov, Woroschilowgrad and Woronesch. A concern that would prove to be justified. A *Fernschreiben* of the LII Army Corps (Freiburg archive) made extensive mention of the '*Befestigungen*' (field fortifications) around Woroschilowgrad.

The *Armeegruppe 'Ruoff'* spoke of several '*Panzergraben*' (tank trenches between two and three metres deep, and between five and seven metres wide), mines on the roads, several rows of barbed wire, electric barricades, bunkers at 100, 150 and 200 metres intervals, of iron and concrete, steel domes of 35 and 45 mm thickness. All this though 'poorly camouflaged', as the LII Corps reported. The latter implied that the Russians had acted hastily, as generally speaking the Soviets were masters of *camouflage*. The electric barricades, a report dated 19.07.1942 (*Gruppe 'Kirchner'*), appeared not to have been connected yet. Here escaped one to an unorthodox weapon.

On 21 May, the results of the counterattack marked themselves on the maps near Kharkov. Suddenly, the Red army no longer wanted to go to Kharkov and Krasnodar, but back across the Donets, to the east. As with Kerch, the attacker became the persecutor. Many could no longer escape and were surrounded. On 29 May 1942, the OKW reported 213,900 prisoners of war, 1,237 tanks destroyed, 1,812 artillery pieces and numerous captured carts and horses. These numbers even had to be revised upwards later. The northern breach of the German front around Woltschansk, after several days' delay due to bad weather, was rolled up through operation '*Fridericus Nord*', also called '*Unternehmen Wilhelm*'.

The astronomical losses gave an insight into the scale on which the war was fought in the east. The battle for Kerch also eventually ended with a Russian loss of 170,000 men in captivity. Additionally, Von Manstein reported 1,133 artillery pieces and 258 annihilated tanks in his memoirs. The losses at Kharkov and Kerch were roughly comparable to the German future losses at Stalingrad. If one then realises that the (unknown) number of casualties at Kerch and Kharkov were not even counted and a considerable number of important battles, some with great losses, would follow for the Red Army, one gets some idea of the sacrifices Russia made.

T-34, Charkov

German troops in the conquered Charkov

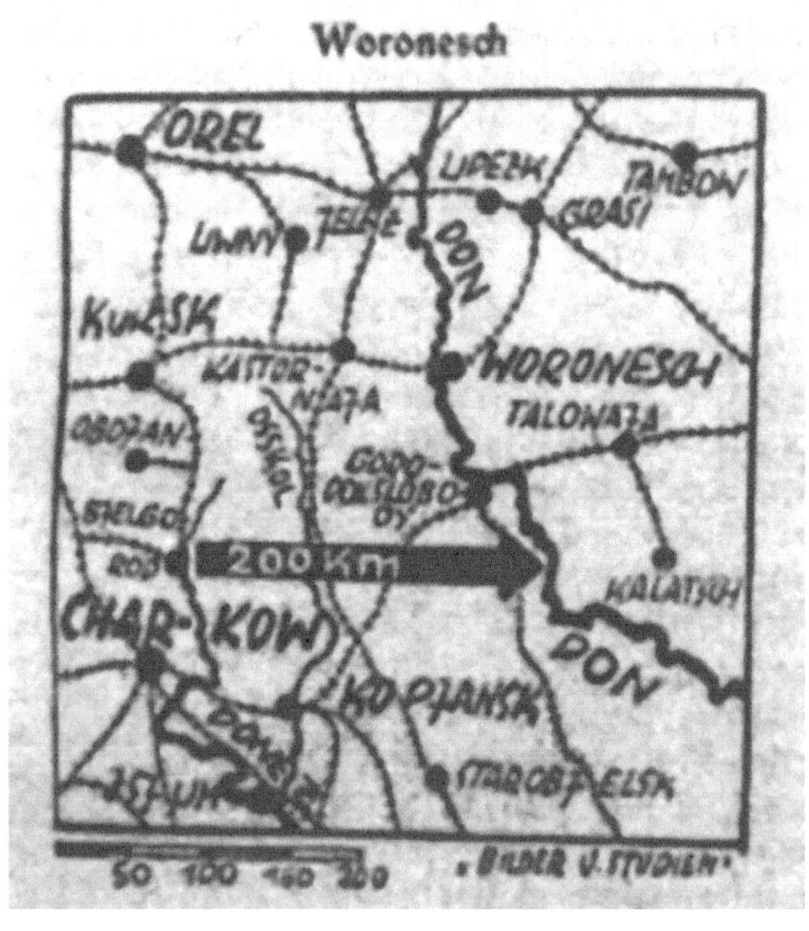

Eastern front to scale, Charkov - Kalatsch

The characteristic highbuilt buildings in the city of Charkov

Charkov in German hands

Disabled KV-tank

German transport, Charkov 1941

Storming Sebastopol

Immediately after Kerch, Operation '*Störfang*', against Sebastopol itself, followed. On 2 June, German troops countered the 100,000-strong Russian garrison. In addition, the Red Army was supported by its fleet operating from the port of Noworossink. Stalin had ordered that Sebastopol should hold out at all costs. A titanic battle began when, on 7 June 1942, the German LIV Corps opened the infantry assault on the city. In this, the Germans were supported by the Romanian army. On 13 June, a number of key Russian fortifications fell into German hands, including 'Fort Stalin' captured by the 22nd Infantry Division, and 'Fort Maxim Gorki-I', which was overrun by the 132nd Infantry Division a day later. Von Manstein achieved results, but the losses were heavy. On 21 June 1942, after capturing new positions, the Sebastopol itself was under direct fire. For the defenders of the city, this was the beginning of the end, although the battle would remain arduous until the last hour, and the Germans had to deploy their heaviest artillery and mortars.

On 29 June, after very heavy aerial bombardments, the final assault was launched. German troops penetrated the city. After initially very heavy fighting, resistance now seemed to collapse rapidly. The Red Army concentrated more and more on individual positions such as the U-Boothaven. The Germans caught radio messages that the Red Army was evacuating its (staff) officers and political commissionaries, leading Von Manstein to conclude that the regular army was being left to fend for itself.

Moreover, thousands of Red Army soldiers were now rushing to the coast, hoping to secure a place on the evacuation ships. By 1 July 1942, 20,000 men had already gathered on a small stretch of beach. A huge chaos ensued. Sebastopol had fallen and Stalin furiously laid the blame on commander Koslow, who had allegedly failed. As many as 95,000 Russians went into captivity. The Germans and Romanians lost about 4,000 men and a multitude of wounded. The number of civilians who had died was very large as well.

Almost simultaneously, the other phase of *Fall Blau -'Weisung nr. 41'* - took effect with Von Bock's attack on the front around Woronesch where the Russian 60th Army was stationed, flanked to the north by the 40th Army (*Brjansk Front*) and to the south by the Russian 6th Army. Here, the ambitions of the German summer offensive of 1942 became visible. Hitler had personally flown to Poltawa on 1 June 1942 to discuss the coming offensive with his officers. Hitler was somewhat frustrated at the delay caused by Russian counter-actions; on the other hand, he suspected that the Soviets had been seriously weakened by their huge losses. Halder, his chief of staff, did not share this view. The talks took place under international pressure. World War II had turned into a real world war, with all its political and diplomatic consequences, and Prague was the scene of the assassination of Hitler's confidant Reinhard Heydrich.

Heeresgruppe Süd wrote its own history. After eliminating the Red Army in the Crimea and the repulsed attack at Kharkov- Ishum and Woltschansk, they now tried to cut off the Russians westward of the Don River with a one-armed encirclement of the hinterland. Yet here, too, things would turn out differently. As at Kerch, the Russians launched fierce counterattacks from the *Brjansk* Front on Von Bock and the border area between *Heeresgruppe 'Süd'* and *'Mitte'*. A clenched unified deployment of the German troops was therefore difficult. And again, as with *'Fridericus'*, a tension arose between the original plan and the reactions needed to the Russian initiatives.

The Russians were well aware of the German plans. During a reconnaissance flight, German staff officer *Major* Reichel's *Fieseler*

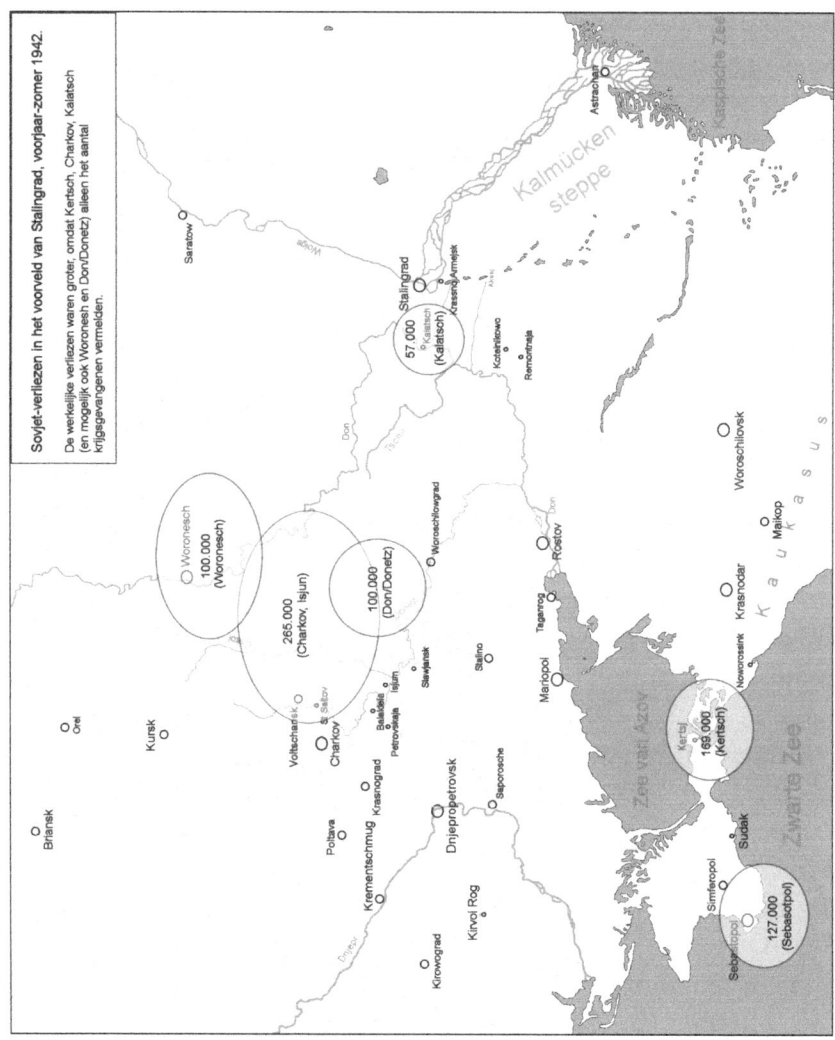

Soviet losses in the front field of Stalingrad, spring-summer 1942. The real losses were bigger, because Kertsch, Charkov, Kalatsch (and possibly Wonoresh and Don/Donetz as well) might just have been reporting the prisoners of war

Storch had been shot down. His briefcase contained *'Fall Blau'*. Reichel's grave was later recovered.

The officer no longer even had his clothes on, so one was sure the Russians now had insight into the plan. Be that as it may, Woronesch was doggedly defended from day one. Despite extensive artillery shelling and aerial bombardments, the German-Hungarian troops met dogged resistance. The city was a strategic road junction. On 30 June, the third day of the offensive, the 24th German Armoured Division got into heavy fighting. At the seam with the *Brjansk Front*, the Russians were now pumping fresh troops into the battle. Marshal Federenk tried to cut off the one-armed encirclement of the Germans, from a northern direction, with a counterattack. However, the Soviet advance came to a halt in the face of fire from the 24th Pz.Division, the armoured grenadier division '*Grossdeutschland*' and smaller units.

Attack and counterattack alternated. Final battle in the Crimea, attack on the Woronesch, swinging to the south, defending to the north as well as Paul's attack (second step '*Blau*') now followed each other in quick succession. The 6th German Army stepped out of its positions on 30 June 1942. The advance succeeded, as did rolling up the front west of the Don. Still, the big operational goals, to capture and destroy the Russian field army, failed to materialise. The perusal of *'Fall Blau'* eventually led Stalin to abandon his current defences and start taking advantage of the country's operative depth. New German operations in the Don region were a blow thereafter, although more than 80,000 Russians were still made prisoners of war. However, the '*Entscheidungsschlacht*', a decisive turning point as Schlieffen and Moltke had always taught *'das Militär'*, did not materialise.

The disabled set 'Maxim' at the Krim

Remnants of the garrison at the Krim gather for surrender

Storm of the Soviet bunkers, Krim 1942

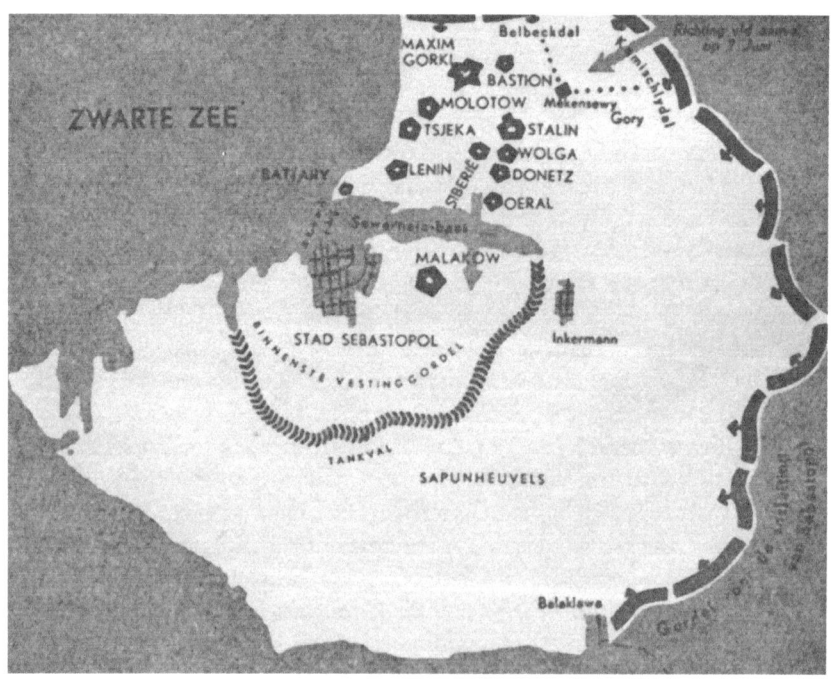
Soviet fortifications at the Krim

11th Army, Krim 1942

The 11th German Army at Sebastopol

Heavy German artillery fired at the Soviet fortifications at Sebastopol

Surrender of the Red Army in Sebastopol

Krim shield

Von Manstein, conquor of the Krim

Crashed IL-2, Shturmovik, July 1942

Ruins of Sebastopol

Von Richthofen, his Stuka units played a major part at Sebastopol and Kertsj

Summer 1942

Soviet prisoners of war

Soviet prisoners of war at Sebastopol

Sebastopol

Soviet anti-aircraft guns Sebastopol Juni 1942

Fort Kertsj

General Von Manstein and staff – Krim

Drawing, German infantry at Perekop

The Red Army lost 127,000 men at Sebastopol

Conquered Soviet bunkers at the Krim

The Krim in German hands

Rostov, bridge over the river Don

Street fight in Rostov

At the border of Asia, at the place of Sporny

Soldiers of the 13 Pz D. in Rostov

Intersection in Rostov after German conquest

March in the Caucasus

Caucasus valley of the Koeban

German soldier in the Caucasus

The supply lines became longer and longer, Caucasus 1942

Difficult circumstances Caucasus 1942

Kluchor-pass, Caucasus 1942 (2816 meter)

Koeban, General Lanz

Railway track Caucasus – Stalingrad

The 'Merciless Battle' for the Danube Metropolis of Rostov - the Gateway to the Caucasus

Timoshenko, the Russian commander in the area, had successfully carried out the strategic retreat. Even the encirclement of the Danube metropolis of Rostov, the final part of the operation *(Blau III)*, which began at Woronesch, did not yield decisive results. Nevertheless, Rostov itself was fanatically defended, including by Russian security units - the NKVD - which had fortified the city with bunkers, barricades and Spanish horsemen. The bridges in the city had been blown up. The *Kriegstagebuch* of the *XXXXIX.Geb.Corps* (archive Freiburg: 22.07.1942) read: *Prisoners tell that Rostov is full of mines. Driving on the roads is forbidden. Only one road is mine-free and on which traffic is allowed. Both the railway station and another large building in the city have been mined. In the streets there are mines in front of every barricade.*

The unpublished diary of Lieutenant Ernst Günther Erner of the 13th Pz.Division (killed 3 February 1944) captured the atmosphere of those days well;

'*Rostov - the sting word has been dropped. Our division had been engaged against the city once already, in late November 1941. Then, because of the sudden onset of winter, the division had to fall back to Taganrog. Throughout the winter we did not forget that. Now we have to storm Rostov for the second time. The 'oldies' know what that means. However, they are keen to take the city this time. At any cost. The marks left by the harsh winter have been very heavy, but slowly forgotten. [...] On dusty roads we drive past endless fields of sunflowers and maize in blistering heat. By noon we crossed the Mius. Nothing can be seen of the enemy [...] We rest in a village, the weapons are cleaned, 'Aufsitzen, Marsch'. [...] We ride through the night. The marching column indicates the direction: East! [...] Our brave Panzer-regiment 4, an Ostmärkisch regiment, advances together with the 'Panzer comrades' of SS-Div.'Wiking'. Staffly approaching the tank ditches of the Russians. By the Stukas and artillery, they are shot storm-ready. Whatever still offers resistance is destroyed or captured. We fight from the vehicles, always driving, always fighting. The same situation at the second tank trench and at the third. Explosions fill the air. All villages are on fire. Large stretches of steppe are also on fire. Above us the Luftwaffe is constantly present. The German eagle is the undisputed master of the sky. The sun disappears at the western 'Heimat' horizon like a fireball. Arriving at the top of a hill, we see the towers of Rostov in the twilight. In this, for us unforgettable, historical moment, I write a letter to my father from my vehicle. My hand is shaking a little, because this afternoon I still had a fever of 39 degrees because of the flu. Physically I am very tired, but mentally and morally I am still thoroughly healthy.*

My thoughts go back to exactly a year ago, when I was wounded in hand-to-hand combat at Fastow. [...] Coffee and food are handed out, and we confidently take up position in front of the town. [...] At it continues, 'fertig machen!', shells of all kinds of calibre descend on Rostov. The city is shot storm-proof. By 05.00 it's forward with our tanks, the decisive phase around Rostov has begun. Bullets fly over our heads, the first wounded. [...]. Rostov airfield is taken at 09.00. Onward we go in oppressive heat. The uniform sticks to the body, beads of sweat stand on the head under the Stahl helmet. [...] but a fantastic strength of will drives us all, everyone keeps up bravely. Every time I think I am at the end of my physical strength, the fever persists, but every time it goes forward. Man has a 'safety valve' and it slams shut when things really don't go on. [...]

Our second company commanded by Feldwebel Weiss captured the bridge over the Don in hand-to-hand combat. Now on to the Great Don Bridge. [...]. At vast open terrain, bullets are raining down. My

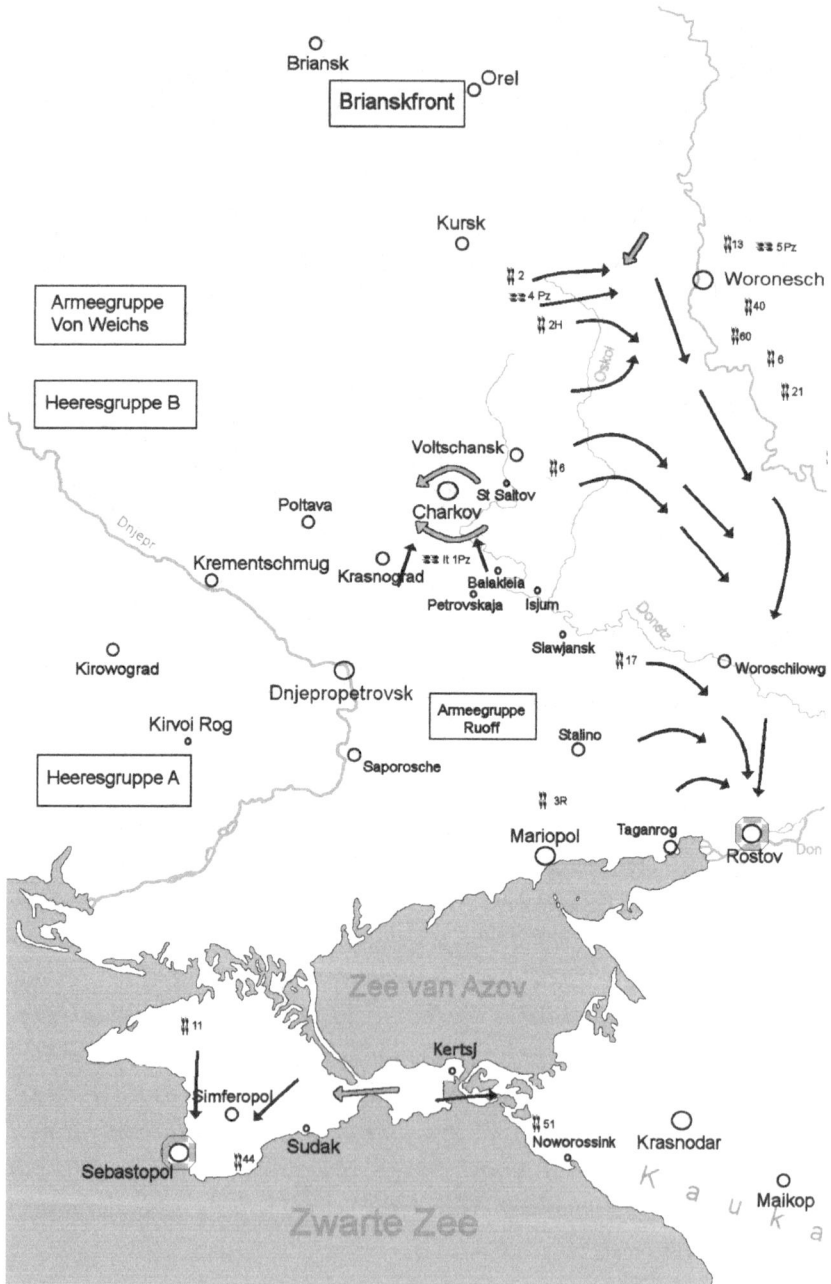

company commander Oberleutnant Schreyer receives a belly shot. Many wounded. All hell has broken loose. The wounded are removed under cover of tanks. One by one, the resistance nests are smoked out. We get closer and closer to the big Don bridge. By evening, when it is finally less warm, an ear-splitting explosion is heard. The Great Don Bridge has been blown up and plunged into the Don. Our brains cannot comprehend what our eyes see.'

Units of the 13th Pz.Division, the '*Wiking*' Division and the 73rd and 298th Infantry Division (I.D.) took the city after a 50-hour battle. Historian Carl Wagener characterised the battle as 'a merciless battle'. Timoshenko's retreat at Woronesch was paid for with a lot of blood, though. Anyone who reads the war diary of the *Oberkommando der Wehrmacht* (OKW) will be surprised with what relentless and unimaginative violence the Russians stormed the German positions near Woronesch day after day. Soviet losses ran so high here that the German commanders wanted to exploit this result by breaking through east at Woronesch and taking the town. Hitler had to point out, with some justification, that the tactical success at Woronesch should not interfere with strategic planning, the turn-in to the south- east. On 3 July, he explicitly informed his generals that Woronesch was not an objective for him. On 4 July, he himself issued a ban on attacking the town when Von Bock could not resist the fat booty. The hunger was possibly fuelled by the reports of the huge booty around Sebastopol, which became known that day. Finally, too few and too late, German units turned in to the south, which was blocked by fuel shortages. The latter was worrying, as after all, the German summer offensive was only a few days old. In short, too little and too late was the motto in the German 'battle in the air'. That Russian losses were nevertheless astronomical was mainly due to their tough, unimaginative and relentless counter-offensives at Kerch, Kharkov and Woronesch. At the last place, the Soviets had fielded 1,800 tanks, half of which the OKW reported on 13 July 1942 had already been destroyed. Infantry losses will always be difficult to ascertain, but it was estimated that the Red Army lost another 100,000 men here.

Hitler feverishly calculated that the Red Army had lost 80 or so divisions in a short time. Who was left to block the road to the east?

With the capture of Crimea, the Donbow and Rostov, a new phase began for *Heeresgruppe Süd*. Hitler was disappointed with the results and Von Bock was replaced. The future offered opportunities, but also dangers. The German armies were now 2,500 kilometres away from home and scattered over a front no less than 1,200 kilometres in length. Logistically alone, this produced a fragile whole. The road network was weak and provisioning was mainly by rail, with the cities of Kharkov and Stalino as bottle necks. Ten German armies had to be supplied via vulnerable supply lines. The German troops constantly had to economise. Fuel in particular was tight, as we already saw between Don and Donets. Stalingrad veteran General Hans Doerr stressed that a strategic momentum had been lost as a result.

The German army now faced a major *dilemma*. The city of Stalingrad and the Volga beckoned, but the Caucasus presented itself. This did mean two different attack targets and a division of the German forces into two different thrust directions: eastward (Stalingrad) and southeastward (Caucasus). On 23 July 1942, Hitler presented *'Führer-Weisung No 45'*. This plan effectuated the division of the southern army group into *Heeresgruppe* (army group) *A*: with the *'Armeegruppe Ruoff'* (17th Army and the 3rd Romanian Army) to attack the western Caucasus (Black Sea coast and the Batum oil area), and furthermore the 1st Army and 4th Pz. Army which were to target the oil fields near Baku and Grozny, the central part of the Caucasus with Tiflis as the provisional final objective.

Heeresgruppe B was to advance eastwards towards Stalingrad from the Don Front, which was to be retained partly as a defensive position. To this end, the 6th Army was deployed. The Russian front between Woronesch along the Don via the Volga past Stalingrad to Astrachan, through the Kalmückensteppe, was to be taken.

New Directions of Advance: Führer-Weisung no 45

No additional troops were available for this new decision and the division of troops into two new army groups with different punching directions. For the upcoming operations, the Germans had about 93 divisions available. Some of these consisted of Romanian and Hungarian units that were not of the same quality as the German troops. If one converted it into combat quality, by the time of *Führer-Weisung No 45*, they were in fact six divisions weaker than at the beginning of the summer conquest and the front troops were even further from home since then. In the summer of 1942, despite all the heavy losses, the Red Army still possessed a formidable armed force. German military intelligence, the '*Abteilung Fremde Heere Ost*', calculated that the Russians had 789 units in the field with the size of a division or brigade, including 407 division-sized infantry units, 178 infantry brigades, 39 cavalry divisions and 165 tank brigades. Converted to divisional strengths, this was 593 divisions.

All this was the prelude to the crisis of Stalingrad. The 6th Army and its allies advanced through the vast Russian landscape between Don and Volga. It was a shadowless flat land, intersected with '*balkas*', a kind of huge gullies, where temperatures could reach 40°C. Dusty roads and sand storms alternated. There was a constant lack of drinking water. A small village popped up every 30 kilometres in this sparsely populated region.

In winter, therefore, the area was very inhospitable. Tem- perature fluctuations of 20°C in a few hours were no exception. Firewood was not at hand. Storms were, with a northeast wind cutting through everything.

Barely a week after Hitler's *'Weisung 45',* Stalin made his emotional appeal on 31 July to 'not concede another inch of ground' to the Germans. At that time, the 6th Army was moving forward towards the Don River, as the main force of *Heeresgruppe B* (Von Weichs), consisting of the *XIV. Pz.Korps,* and Army Corps XI, VII, and LI plus allies. As a prelude to Stalin's call to battle, the 4th Pz.Army (Hoth) which had initially turned south from the northern Millerovo area towards the Caucasus - as part of *Heeresgruppe A* (List) - had been recalled by Hitler and added as a southern spearhead towards Kalatsch- Stalingrad and Volga. The shuffling of this important unit, which had been the subject of earlier debate at Woronesch, indicated that the Germans were constantly vacillating between tactics and strategy, struggling with wishful thinking and unruly reality. People simply wanted too much with too few unities. Shuffling was the result, as was wasted time.

Indeed, the 6th Army (Paulus) was too weak to complete the advance to Stalingrad alone. After all, it had barely been 60 days since it had had to repel the attack of a much larger army (Ti-Moshenko) in the vicinity of Kharkov, and even after that it had been constantly active in the Donets basin. While Hitler pointed out the usefulness of Germany's allies, not everyone was so convinced of their qualities. Von Rundstedt believed after the war, Antony Beevor wrote, that the Italians were 'terrible people', the 'Hungarians wanted to go home quickly' and the Romanian officers were 'below standard'. Only the Romanian mountain troops were accorded any quality.

In practice, it now meant that the 6th Army approached Sta- lingrad from the north-west, while the 4th Army, which was already south of the Don River due to operations within the *Heeresgruppe A* area, attacked Stalingrad from the south-west. The *Luftflotte 4* supported the battle from the air. Stalingrad increasingly became the epicentre of the force measurement.

Initially, the 6th Army managed to gain ground. The army was divided into two assault groups, with a north wing consisting of the

XIV. Pz.Corps, the VIII and XVII Army Corps, and in the south the LI Army Corps reinforced by armoured units. However, there were already hefty warnings: the north wing was meeting increasing resistance from Stalingrad, and the southern group could only advance by drawing on units from the 4th Pz.Army. On 23 July, when Hitler decided that *Heeresgruppe A* should be given priority with supplies of ammunition and fuel, the advance came to a halt for eight days. Hitler expressed his wish that the right wing of *Heeresgruppe A* in particular should be given sufficient fuel to advance to the Black Sea. The 4th Pz.Army battled its way from the south via Remontnaja (3 August) to Arkssai (7 August) and from there with the *XXXXVIII. Pz.Korps* towards Krassno Armejsk, just south of Stalingrad, on the Volga, which they reached at the end of August.

Red Army Defends Stalingrad at Kalatsch - the Last Classic Battle of Encirclement in the East

The Red Army had another surprise *in store* before the battle of Stalingrad began. With the German army stalled for more than a week due to fuel shortages, Russian command had decided to hold out in the Kalatsch bridgehead, westward of the Don, and resist the German army like a battle of Borodino (1812). This was entirely in line with Stalin's orders of holding out. Once again, German plans were thwarted. Think of the difference if the Germans had been able to attack simultaneously with the 6th Army and 4th Pz.Army and there had been sufficient fuel and ammunition. Stalingrad would then already have been taken in the pincers. Still, history is not about 'if'; there was renewed fighting - such as at Kharkov, Woronesch (the Russian counterattacks continued there even in August 1942), Sebastopol and Kerch - and experience has shown that this involved everyone paying their lessons in blood.

The battle at Kalatsch was special in many ways. Paulus conducted a classic concentric attack there. It was the final phase of the characteristic German '*Blitzkrieg*' in which the enemy was surrounded and defeated in concentric attacks by cooperating armoured, infantry and air units. Yet it was also where the Red Army, 12 infantry divisions and five armoured brigades strong, gained time once again. Additionally, as usual, the decisive fighting started with a *pre-emptive strike* by the Red Army on 31 July, towards the Golubinskaya hills, on the northern flank of the Kalatsch bridgehead that ran from Katschalinsky on the north side, west of Sstanin in the centre, and had the Tschir and Don as its southern flank around Werch-Schirskaya. It produced fierce fighting. The Russians managed to increase their bridgehead, but there was no strategic turnaround. On 7 August 1942, the 6th Army had sufficient fuel and ammunition again, and concentric attacks could be launched. Here, the 6th Army showed that its teeth were still sharp. The strong Soviet force was split apart and a formidable German victory was already emerging on 10 August. The OKW's war diary noted on 11 August 1942 that the western Don bank at Kalatsch had been cleared, after the 16th and 24th Pz.Divisions had reached out to each other a few days earlier. The next day the first reports of the results arrived:

35,000 prisoners, 270 tanks and 560 artillery pieces. These were units of the Russian 62nd Army and 1st Pz.Army. The number of POWs would rise to over 50,000 more.

8,8 cm flak, 16 Inf. D. in the Kalmückensteppe

Kalmückensteppe, signpost of the 16 Inf. D. (mot.) between Elista and Jaschkul-Utta-Chalchutta

Drink water storage16 inf. D. at Jaschkul

German losses - Kalmückensteppe

Civilians fleeing, Steppe August 1942

Kalmückensteppe, disabled T-34 tank with fallen crew

Soviet soldiers, Kalatsch 1942

Soviet soldiers, captured at Kalatsch, in the camp at Pokrowkij

Soviet tank battle – Steppe 1942 Millerowo

Disabled T-34

March in the Steppe. Disabled T-60 tank

Soviet infantry tried to stop the German 6th Army at Kalatsch

Disabled Soviet T-34 tank, Kalmückensteppe

On route to the city at the Wolga

Before Kalatsch 1942

Damaged Soviet transport

Target Stalingrad and the First Problems for the German Attackers

Aerial photographs of Stalingrad showed that hundreds of ferry-boats were ready on the Volga banks. Most of the bridges had been destroyed. Would the Russians give up on the city? It looked like they had fired their last shot at Kalatsch. The Sixth Army pushed East. The flanks on which the allies mainly operated grew longer and longer. The Germans were not quite blind to the danger posed by this. One tried to free infantry units from other fronts to support the allies in the second line and the hinterland as flank protection. However, the '*overstretch*' of German army groups moving at right angles to each other was drawing dangerously. The results in the Caucasus were spectacular on paper. A huge amount of ground was gained. Moreover, in a short time (01.07- 10.08.1942), more than 300,000 men had been made prisoners of war, more than 500 Soviet tanks destroyed and the oil fields of Maikop were up for grabs. Fuel experts were on standby in Rostov, but bad news came. The oil fields and installations had been skilfully damaged by the Russians. The decisive battle again failed to materialise; after every German victory, new units faced them. Hitler became irritated by such reports of Russian troop strength, dismissing them as defeatism.

And so it continued. On 15 August, the 6th Army again put in motion. North of Kalatsch, a bridgehead was built out on the east bank of the Don; two more bridgeheads followed at Peskowatka and Wertjatschij on 22 August. The next day, at 5pm, the historic news came in that the 6th Army was on the Volga River. The 4th Pz.Army, which again faced fuel shortages (19 August, 23 August), followed from the south. Stalingrad was surrounded.

Around that historic moment, 25 August 1942, the *Generalquartiermeister*, *Generalleutnant* Wagner, warned *Führer* headquarters that the supply lines of *Heeresgruppe A* and *B* were out-of-control. He explained that with the approaching wet season, the so-called '*raspudica*', and then winter, supplies had to be delivered via the railway lines more and more. However, these were not yet fully available in this area. Russian track was 8.9 centimetres wider than the German rail network, and this had to be converted. A Russian railway also had significantly fewer sleepers than a German one, and even Russian coal - from the conquered coal mines of the Donets basin - was suitable for the more modern German locomotives only after being mixed with German coal. The German railways had to make ongoing modifications to run their locomotives. The equipment was so sensitive, that at the beginning of the war during the winter 70% of trains were already stranded at Brest-Litowsk. *Reichsverkehrsminister* Dorpmüller had then spared no expense to improve matters. Every day, 40 to 50 trains rolled through Rostov alone in the autumn of 1942, before the war in the Caucasus. Yet in the newly conquered areas, the railways were simply not ready. Wagner advised that shuttles should be set up, using trucks to move supplies between the damaged and not yet rebuilt stretches of track. On 21 August, the first report of snowfall was sent from the Caucasus to *Heeresgruppe A*. In addition, Hitler was constantly worried about a possible Allied landing in the west. To this end, two important divisions, the '*Leibstandarte Adolf Hitler*' and '*Grossdeutschland*', had been cleared for deployment in the west in the past few weeks. These were reserves that were now no longer available on the eastern front. And the 11th Army was not released for the southern front, but was directed towards Leningrad. A cumbersome *manoeuvre* that, moreover, given the advancing year, would no longer have any decisive impact.

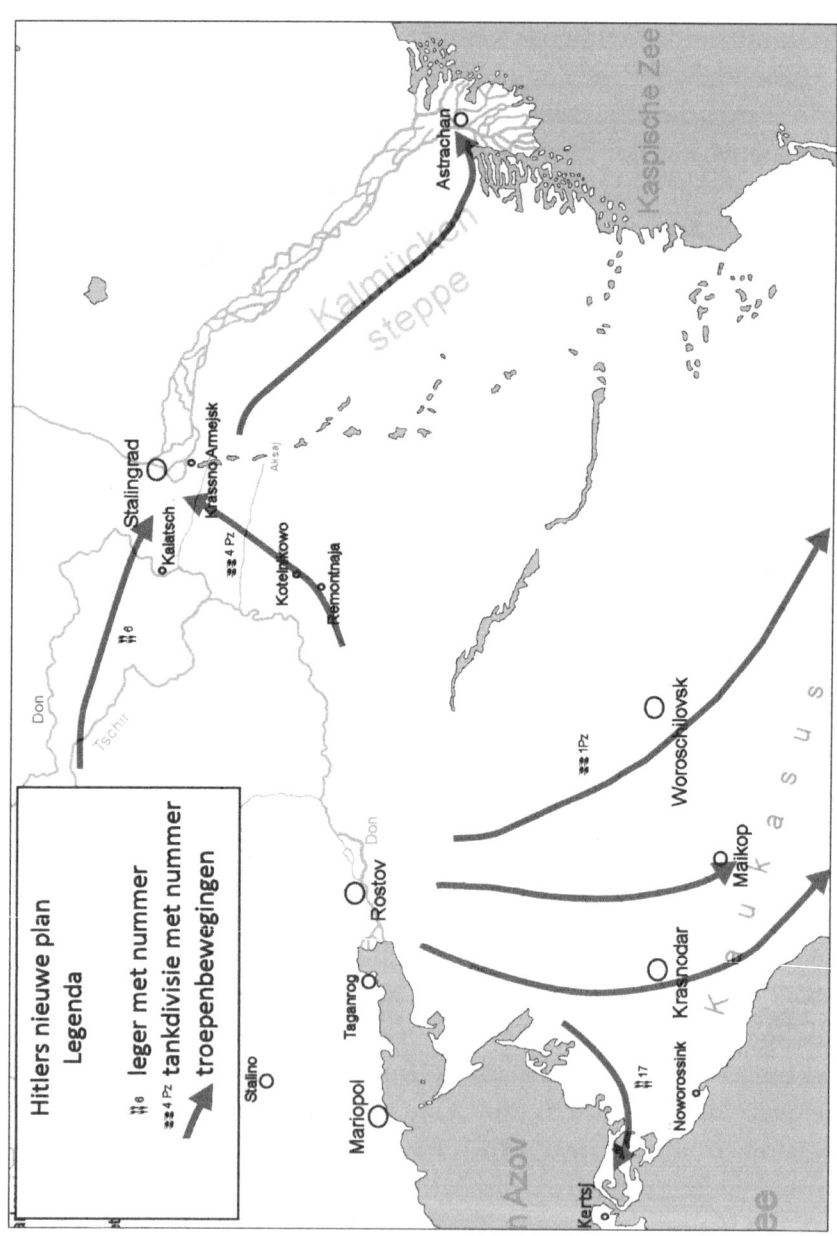
Operationplan 1942

Treeless area

Starting up the coal mines in the Donetz area was also far from easy. *Generalmajor* Von Clae, commander of the *Oberfeldkommandantur 397*, was in charge of this and had been assigned Russian POWs: 2,000 men from '*Dulag*' (*Durchgangslager*) *180;* Staff Officer 'OKW' Wilhelm Keitel had promised 30,000 in the summer. Furthermore, this required supporting guard units, including Cossack troops. The 111th I.D. had had to temporarily cede trucks for the start-up period. Von Clae operated in the Gorlowka- Dsershinsk area. In a report on the *Ingangsetzung des Berg- baues* (mine exploitation) *im Donez-Gebiet*, it was pointed out to him that the army, too, would need coal, if one was to be 'in treeless territory this winter', by which, of course, the steppe around Stalingrad was meant. However, the mines had been rendered unusable and (Russian) specialists were not available.

In another internal report of the *LVII. Pz.Corps*, dated 14 July 1942, had already noted serious deficits in many areas. The corps stressed that Germany could only succeed with an '*eiserne Sparsamkeit*'. This had to be 'instilled' in every soldier. 'Without a doubt, our food situation is in a bad way,' said the report, which mentioned the increasing dexterity of the Russians in working with landmines (activatable on standby) too, as well as the use of so-called 'German' road signs stating that the area was 'mine-free', when in reality it was dangerous territory. The *LVII. Pz.Corps* ordered its own signs with divisional signs as a countermeasure. Furthermore, they increasingly feared the use of gas: 'It is conceivable that the Russians, now that they are drowing, reach for the drug gas [...] the troops must be prepared that it could come to a gas war. You must state unequivocally that our masks protect the men.' Lack of food and the resulting fatigue and apathy among the troops, were a growing problem as well. Weary troops tried to ride along on the already overloaded panje wagons (supply wagon with a horse in front of it). *Generaloberst* Ruoff reported: 'Several times it has been observed that soldiers were riding along on overloaded and fully loaded panje wagons. This was not allowed. I cannot point this out strongly enough.'

They were signs on the wall and it would all get much worse.

Betrayal?

During these same historic August days, there was another matter that still raises questions today: the operation and relocation of the *XXXXVIII. Pz.Corps* of General Heim. In the recent study *'Verrat an der Ostfront',* Friedrich Georg questioned whether there was malice here, treachery. The units of the *XXXXVIII. Pz.Corps* had first thrust northward from the area north of Abganerowo on the Akssaj River, only to turn around at Tundutowo, take the same route southward again, and counter Stalingrad further west (east of Sety) via Gawrilowaka, Zybenko and Bassargino. Georg found this an incomprehensible action, given that the army group was struggling with fuel shortages and this *manoeuvre* involved almost 100 kilometres of diversions. Friedrich Georg now argues that the 4th Pz.Army in fact had little weather in front of it, because otherwise it could not afford to take the *XXXXVIII. Pz.Corps* away and move it to the *LI. Corps*. The lack of Soviet resistance would have been confirmed at a staff meeting on 23 August attended by Hoth, the Commander of *Luftflotte 4* Von Richthofen, and the Commander *Generaloberst* Von Weichs of *Heeresgruppe B*. This would have demonstrated 'treachery'.

Was there really treason though, and by whom and how? Closer examination nevertheless provides a different, more nuanced picture. On 24 August, the OKW war diary reported that there was a disagreement about how to proceed with the 4th Pz.Army. Soviet units had been dispersed and the 4th Pz. Army wanted to consolidate the position and clear the enemy remnants first. The *Heeresgruppe* on the other hand wanted one to break through immediately. Following this, there are somewhat conflicting reports; on the 25th, it was reported that 'the (Soviet) attacks on the 4th Pz.Army were weakening', only to conclude on 26 August that 'the 4th Pz.Army is making no progress'.

The obvious explanation for this variety of conclusions is the poorly functioning German military intelligence services, which had trouble with time schedules. In fact, they often reacted almost *ad hoc* to what happened at the front. This 'daily rate' naturally fluctuated a lot. It seems most plausible that the *Heeresgruppe* simply wanted to move on quickly before the Russians recovered, and opted for a compromise: the *XXXXVIII. Pz.Corps* (after Hoth first hesitated and then put down the opposition) was to move south and then deploy more westwards. At that point, after all, the 6th Army was having good successes. Kalatsch had been completely cleared by 29 August, and on the north side of Stalingrad, German units had already entered the city. One wanted to close the pincers on the Volga bank as soon as possible.

That the situation on the eastern wing of the 4th Pz.Army was indeed deteriorating was confirmed by the OKW on 28 August, when increasing pressure on 'the right wing' of the 4th Pz.Army was reported. Specialist books on the Soviet side, such as those by John Erickson, have ignored the *manoeuvre* of the *XXXXVIII. Pz.Corps*, but there seems to be no betrayal here; rather a somewhat nervous shuffling with limited resources. Hans Doerr, at the time attached to the *VII. Corps* and later liaison officer with the 4th Romanian Army, argued that the complications at the *XXXXVIII. Pz.Corps* stemmed from Soviet resistance: 'Just 20 km from Stalingrad, the army came to a standstill.' In the process, the tank units were isolated. The infantry, predominantly Romanian units, had been left behind despite their good will. Tanks, after all, could not go on endlessly solo without sufficient infanterial support, as they would get into trouble during enemy flank attacks. The failed German disengagement offensive from Kotelnikowo would demonstrate this in the near future, but previous deployments in the east - such as the 'forced halt' of the tank units (Hoepner) of *Heeresgruppe Nord*, on the Luga River - had made this clear. The same was true when entering the prepared defensive positions around Stalingrad. It should also be remembered that the final jump to the city outskirts went through hills, between Krassnoarmejsk and Beketowka, which were defended as the southern flank of Stalingrad. Isolated tank units that had to advance via hill routes were very vulnerable. The best example of this was seen on the Eastern Front in January 1945, when the *IV. SS Pz.Corps,* with two tank divisions ('*Totenkopf*' and '*Wiking*'), tried to reach the enclosed city of Budapest via the Gerecse-Pilis mountains. Via anti-tank positions (with Pak) and road closures here, the advance around the towns of Zsámbék and Bickske was severely frustrated. Budapest was not relieved.

Finally, Friedrich Georg's treachery thesis is further weakened when we look at the units directly involved in the field. Rittmeister Rolf Grams wrote the divisional history of the 14th Pz.Division involved in these battles. This mentions very heavy fighting with Russian tank units that had *T-34* tanks. In the uncovered steppe before the hill country, the German tanks of *Pz.Rgt. 36* were no longer in the forefront. That things were tough right from the start was shown by the fact that of the 200 tanks with which the division entered the field, only 24 were still deployable by 10 August. The Red Army lost 70 *T-34s* here. Most of the tanks of *Pz.Rgt. 36* were in repair workshops in Aksay. On 20 August, Grams reported two days of fighting in which 'the whole division was put in the scales'. *Stukas* arrived as the battle turned to Prywolsky and Tinguta station. 'The attack was again stalled; an attempt to get more air north at Morosoff failed'. In short, the relocation of the *XXXXVIII. Pz.Corps* was not without reason and even within the new lines of attack further west, the corps regrouped several times. The German troops simply lacked the men and strength to take massive action. Like water, they sought the lowest point, and there they pressed on.

The Battle of Stalingrad

Stalingrad (now: Wolgograd) was an elongated city on the west bank of the Volga River. To the north, the city was flanked by the towns of Rynok and Spartakowka, followed by the tractor factory in the northern part of the city, the *'Barrikade'* (*Barikady*) gun factory, the bread factory, the *'Red October'* metal-working company, the *Lazur* chemical plant and the connecting road that became known (because of its shape) as the 'tennis racket'. In the centre were: the Mamai Kurgan hill, the main railway station, the department store and Red Square; and in the *'Altstadt'* (southern part) station south and the silo with its striking silhouette. To the south, Stalingrad was flanked by the town of Kuporosnje.

Stalingrad had become a major manufacturing centre in Soviet times. Its favourable location in the Volga knee meant that coal from the Donets basin could easily be transported by boat across the Volga to other industrial centres. There were also good rail connections to Moscow and the Caucasus. Furthermore, Stalingrad was an important refining centre and transshipment point for oil from the south. While oil went north, wood came south, for the treeless steppes. The city's factories were, together with those of Kharkov and Chelyabinsk, among the largest in the country. The tractor factory (*'Djerzinski'*) was kept running by as many as 12,000 workers. Stalingrad was also one of the cities where the most tanks (250 *T-34* per month) and artillery (100 guns per month) were produced. With all these activities, the city had grown from 150,000 inhabitants to half a million between 1926 and 1939.

What followed after the battle of Kalatsch and the regroupments was itself miraculous. Where Hitler starved Leningrad, pulverised Sebastopol with artillery and forbade entering Woronesch, the 6th Army and the 4th Pz.Army were sucked into Stalingrad like a magnet. All hitherto followed theories were abandoned. For the Germans, it was the outcome of the ultimate *'overstretch'* of their capabilities. Like between fatally tired boxers, it was here that things had to be decided. Fuel, combat power and units were lacking to operate broadly for longer. And as the city became more central to the messaging, its symbolism and prestigious increased too. Stalingrad, the city that barely played a role at the start of *'Fall Blau'*, became the focal point of the 1942 summer offensive an offensive that would slip into winter.

Gone were the manoeuvres in the Don and Volga knees. The battle centred on a city that had been mercilessly bombed by *Luftflotte 4*. By some estimates, as many as 40,000 people, mostly civilians, had been killed in the massive initial aerial bombing. The Germans slowly fought their way through a packed industrial city with the appearance of a ruin. The city still contained many Russian civilians who, following Stalin's orders, were not allowed to step back either. There are reports of Russian elite units mercilessly shooting retreating civilians. The ferries were used exclusively for the Red Army. When eventually a boat did take in civilians, it was hit by grenate and sank. The army ferries did not sail out to rescue them and German soldiers asked their officers if they could help the civilians with their *pontoons*. The leadership forbade this. They did decide not to fire on the wretches who had managed to save themselves on an island in the river. This did not happen even when they were picked up days later. Occasionally, there was a flurry of humanity.

Still, the hard truth was that a no-holds-barred war of attrition was going on in Stalingrad. The East Prussian 24th Pz.Division bled to death at *'Barrikade'*, *'Lazur'* and the tennis racket (18.10.1942); the grenadiers of the 389th I.D. died *en masse* at the *Djerzinski* tractor factory where Russian *T-34* tanks were made, and later penetrated

'*Red Barrikade*' (14.10.1942). The Baden-Württemberg 305th I.D. fought to the death with Colonel Gurtjev's Russian 308th I.D. for possession of the tractor factory (24.10.1942). Additionally, there was heavy fighting in the suburbs. Snipers and artillery held the city in a deadly grip. At a strategic crossroads, it was hit every time. German reinforcements and ammunition and weapons transports came under constant fire. A Croatian unit, also stationed in Stalingrad, discovered that the Soviets had an observation post in the chimney of a factory. A '*Sturmgeschütz*' (cannon on tracked undercarriage) of the *Sturmgeschüt- zabteilung 224* commanded by *Oberkanonier* Walter Kretz was brought into position and blasted the chimney to rubble with about five shots. Kretz received a Croatian intercept on the spot. It was an example of the ongoing '*Kleinkrieg*' being waged.

All results notwithstanding, the Germans had failed to capture Stalingrad in a pincer manoeuvre from the north and south. The 4th Pz.Army was stuck in the hills south of Stalingrad and had turned west at Krassnoarmejsk. The 6th Army failed to advance from the north along the Volga bank and also fanned out to the west. So instead of reaching out to each other on the Volga bank, the armies met west of the city. Then they fought their way in head- on. Like two phalanxes, the armies faced each other; a battle of attrition ensued. The Germans succeeded in capturing 9/10 of the city, but the Russians persisted, digging deep into the steep banks of the Volga and a handful of industrial buildings.

October and November were lost to the German attackers without any operative progress. Twice they had launched a large- scale attack, 14 October and 10 November - the latter supported by well-trained pioneer units - against '*Lazur*', the 'tennis racket' and '*Red October*'. One managed to penetrate the buildings, but there was no total conquest. Although Hitler made a constant appeal to the patriotism of his soldiers, his close associates gradually realised that they were at a dead end. Halder had noted in his diary that the 6th Army had actually already entered the city very tired. After eight weeks of fighting in the city, there was no end in sight. The battle had become a defensive war; they no longer counted in kilometres, but in metres. The Russians showed themselves masters of house-to-house fighting and *camouflage*. For the Russians, it was now a matter of holding out with their backs against the Volga, binding the German troops and preparing their countermeasures. Meanwhile, the German 6th Army and 4th Pz.Army were consuming their operative and mobile power in conditions similar to 1914-'18.

Stavka makes plans

In Moscow, the cards were shuffled again. By order of Stalin, his generals Zhukov and Vasilevsky had investigated the possibilities around Stalingrad. Zhukov had personally studied the northern flank, while Vasilevsky had inspected the front in the south. Together they came to the conclusion that there were great operative opportunities on the flanks, where Germany's allies were at the front. The Romanian positions in particular offered opportunities. The Romanians were located with the 4th Army south of Stalingrad (headquarters in Kotelnikowo), and with the 3rd Army (headquarters in Morozovsk) on the north-west flank, running along with the river Don which, via Woronesch, formed the northwest-shifting front line. To the north of the 3rd Romanian Army were the Italians on the Don (8th Army), followed by the 2nd Hungarian Army (north of Pavlovsk). From north to south, the Soviets had the *Woronesch Front* (facing 2nd Hungarian and 8th Italian Armies), the *Southwest Front* (facing 3rd Romanian Army), the Don *Front* (facing 3rd Romanian Army), the *Stalingrad Front* (facing the 6th Army and 4th Pz.Army) while the 51st and 28th Russian Armies were facing the Romanian 4th Army.

What did the Germans know or suspect? This question is not so easy to answer. Regardless of what they knew, their hands were tied. Hitler had already said on 14 October that the positions now held would have to be preserved for a favourable starting position in 1943. The question of how this should then be preserved, he ignored. It was an awkward split in which the Germans found themselves. In fact, they would have to abandon the huge area gains of the summer campaign and retreat behind Don and Tschir, with Rostov as a bridgehead eastwards, to accommodate the coming winter offensive in a shortened defensible front and also to have street reserves again. Moreover, they realised that in 1943, they might not even have the strength to move eastward again on such a large scale and have to occupy or secure even more territory. In the absence of alternatives and troops, they were stuck with the existing fragile situation.

The 6th Army and 4th Pz.Army suspected a Soviet attack tight around the city, to enclose it. Hitler himself expected a deployment with the 3rd Romanian Army and the Italians, while '*Fremde Heere Ost*', whose job it was actually to make such forecasts, suspected that the Red Army would become active near the central front earlier. According to historian Heinz Magenheimer, this misjudgement stemmed from the fact that it was only relatively late that people recognised the positions of the Russian 5th Pz.Army at the *South-West Front*, let alone the 2nd Garda Army, 3rd Garda Army and the 5th Thrust Army in the picture, which were commanded by the *Stavka*. These were the reserves requested by Zhukov and Vasilvsky, which Stalin had released from the *Stavka*'s reserves. Stalin had hidden these reserves from his own generals, lest they think their deployment was the only counterweight against the attackers, and thus he hoped to get the best out of his soldiers. The journalist-historian and contemporary Walter Kerr spoke of 'the secret of Stalingrad' in this sense.

In any case, we can say with certainty that in the first two weeks of November, the OKW faced Soviet actions on its flanks almost daily. This was a serious sign of things to come. To get an insight into the information that reached Hitler and the highest staffs:

2 November: The battle in Stalingrad was paralysed. It was considered to halt attacks in the city for eight days, which Hitler eventually rejected. The 71st I.D. was considered badly beaten. Hitler suspected a major Soviet counterattack. Russian bridgeheads were bombed, and forest plots were attacked at random from the air, because people despised gathered troops there.

3 November: Soviet troops tried to cross the river into the front area of the Romanians, Italians and Hungarians.

4 November: Hitler ordered reinforcements from the west (including the 6th Pz.Division and *306. I.D.*) to the eastern front, to strengthen the ranks of the 3rd Romanian Army and the 8th Italian Army.

6 November: The OKW concluded that *Luftwaffe forces* in the Don arc were too weak, especially in area north and north-west of Stalingrad. Near the Hungarians, the Soviets tried to cross the Don again; at Swoboda, this resulted in an encounter in which 400 Russians were killed.

7 November: Russian attacks south of Stalingrad on the 20th Romanian Division.

8 November: Russian troop concentrations south of Stalingrad were dispersed by German artillery. Near Woronesch again signalled Soviet troop build-up.

10 November: In front of Romanian positions again Soviet troop concentrations. Artillery again chases them apart.

11 November: Soviet attacks on the 1st Romanian Cavalry Division. The Hungarians wage another battle at Swoboda.

12 November: Soviet attack on junction (separation) of the 6th Army and 3rd Romanian Army.

13 November: another landing attempt at Hungarian.

The *Luftwaffe* also signalled the confluence of Russian combat forces. Von Richthofen's diary gives plenty of evidence of this.

13 November 1942: 'The Russians are attacking towns and roads, presumably to prepare for their attack, which will now soon come'.

14 November 1942: 'Deployment against Russian advance at the Don'.

16 November 1942: 'Russian troop concentrations are increasingly approaching the Don. [...] I believe it is preparation for an attack.'

18 November 1942: 'Attack at Romanians by seven Russian bataljons.'

19 November 1942: 'This morning the Russians began the expected major attack on the Don.'

Uranus

It seems a safe conclusion that the Germans themselves also suspected that counter-actions were imminent. When we read in Zhukov's memoirs that the Red Army had no less than 27,000 trucks and 1,300 railway wagons deployed a day to get equipment and men in readiness, then it could not help but have a well-founded suspicion. At most, the sheer scale would surprise Germany.

Countermeasures had been taken, but they were too few and too late. Their own operative reserves directly in the area, the mobile ones of the 6th Army and 4th Pz.Army, were not actually reserves at all, but were partly tied up in the city, too small and already virtually bled dry. These were flags on the map with only limited capabilities.

Operation '*Uranus*', the Soviet counter-offensive, broke loose on Nov 19, after just under a week of 'calm before the storm'. The Soviet's attack began on the northern flank, against the 3rd Romanian Army where the Soviets fielded overwhelming superiority, namely the 1st Guards Army, 5th Tank Army and 21st Army. Altogether 18 infantry divisions, 8 tank brigades, 2 mechanised brigades, 6 cavalry divisions and 1 anti-tank brigade; all commanded by Nicolai Vatutin. This attack was followed a day later by an attack on the 4th Romanian Army south of Stalingrad by the 51st Soviet Army on 20 November 1942.

The Soviet attack became an instant success. This was evidenced by the fact that the spears of both armies met at Kalatsch as early as 23 November 1942. With this, the encirclement of the German army at Stalingrad was a fact, although the ring was still porous at that time. The meteoric collapse of the flanks sparked a bitter historical debate about the German-Romanian brotherhood. Had the Romanians failed?

General Doerr believes such a judgement would be 'un-knightly'. The Romanians had hitherto shown themselves to be loyal allies of the Germans and had had decent achievements in Crimea, the Donets region and the Caucasus. Even in the city of Stalingrad, thousands of Romanians would share the fate of the German soldiers. The Romanians were simply too poorly equipped and had neither heavy artillery nor good anti-tank weapons. The only anti-tank guns available were 3.7 cm guns that the Germans themselves had long since replaced with heavier *Pak* (*Panzerabwehrkanone*). Despite these internal weaknesses, the Romanian divisions did have to spread their strength over 20 kilometres of front length per division, which was considerable. They were, in one word, hopeless.

The Soviet attack against Dumitrescu's 3rd Romanian Army had begun after hours of artillery bombardment. The Soviets mainly attacked the Romanian divisions, which were the most western, in order to stay as far away from the German units as possible. Indeed, the 14th German Pz.Division thrust directly to the west, coming to the aid of the 1st Romanian Cavalry Division. However, the main attack took place with other Romanian divisions. Here, the Russians cut through the lines effortlessly. General Lascar's 15th Romanian I.D., which was between them, was left as an island. In the southern attack against Constantinescu's 4th Romanian Army, the 4th Pz.Army immediately deployed the 29th Div. (mot.), but it could not provide sufficient counterweight. Paulus, the commander of the 6th Army, immediately understood what had happened and signalled to headquarters: 'army enclosed' (22 november 18:00).

Before this report, frantic attempts had been made to turn the tide with Heim's already troubled corps (*XXXXVIII. Pz.Corps*). This corps was already weakened by then, with the attached 22nd Pz.Division mostly with only light tanks, the 1st Romanian Pz.Division with 40 Czech (*Skoda*) tanks that could also pass for 'light'. Nevertheless, they bumped into Soviet units. At the crossing over waterways both divisions lost contact, so they separated at Sirki (the Romanians) and at Medweditsky (the 22nd) met the full weight of the 5th Soviet Pz.Army. Left and right, the *XXXXVIII. Pz.Corps* was also passed by many tank units. Paulus then tried to pull the troops back from this futile battle, the 22nd managed to move westwards - losing contact with the Romanians in the process - but had to swing again to rescue the remaining 15th Romanian I.D. This left the 22nd Pz. Division itself in trouble again and Paulus' only 'major' mobile reserve largely winged, right at the start of the encirclement of the 6th Army.

With the 14th Pz.Division, things were not much different. This division hailing from the Dresden area had been placed as a reserve in the Don arc. This was mainly a paper fact. The division had literally bled to death in the fighting in Stalingrad for the '*Red October*' factory. The divisional chronicler, Grams, pointed out that in one of the reports of the *Pz.Gren.Rgt. 103* (*Oberstleutnant* Seydel) it had to be reported that the combat strength at that time was 1 '*Feldwebel*' (non-commissioned officer) and 28 men. Available for the new operations were parts of the *Pz.Art.Rgt. 4*, the anti-tank troops of *Pz.Jg. Abt. 4*, the liaison troops, some remnants of *Pz.Rgt. 36* and regiments 103 and 108, which were amalgamated into battalions. The motorised (mot.) units moved from fire to fire, taking out several dozen Soviet tanks and a cavalry regiment on 19 and 20 November. But it did not help. The less mobile units that had to hold out without infantry support and tanks were overrun piece by piece, such as the *IV. Pz.Art.Rgt.* with, among others, its precious 8.8 cm. 'Flak' (*FlugabwehrKanone*) which was also used as an anti-tank gun.

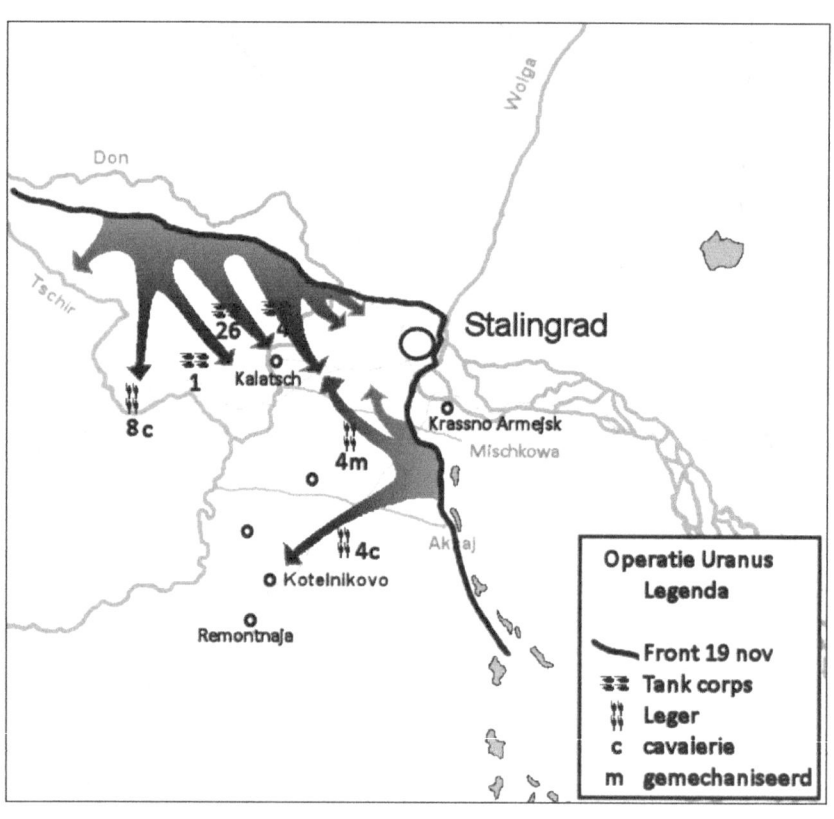

Tanks of the 6th Pz. D., Pz.Rgt.11. This unit operated with extreme care, wich caused a loss of valuable time

Bridge over the Aksaj

Operation Wintergewitter Sd Kfz 221

Radical Measures are Needed - but Paulus is Bound by Politics

At the *Heeresgruppe,* they immediately realised that things were serious. As early as 19 November, the first day of the offensive, Von Weichs believed that these Russian attacks called for 'radical measures'. One of these was that German assault operations in Stalingrad were immediately halted and units, especially of the *XIV. Pz.Corps*, were released to serve as operative reserves. The loss of the site and especially river crossing at Kalatsch was very serious. A small German garrison had been overpowered by surprise, when one suspected own troops instead of Russian units. Only a bridge at Perepolny and Akimolvsky, defended by the 384th I.D., now offered hope towards the west. However, Hitler was already drawing very different conclusions; on the night of 21-22 November 1942, he gave the ominous order to establish a *Festung 'Stalingrad'*. This meant standing firm, not giving up any territory. Hitler also soon gave the impetus for the establishment of a new *Heeresgruppe,* the *Heeresgruppe 'Don'* (3rd Romanian Army, 6th Army, 4th Pz.Army, 4th Romanian Army), with reinforcements by parts of the 11th Army. Troops coming from other fronts such as the already mentioned 6th Pz.Division, as well as the 11th Pz.Division, would also be directed eastwards with even more urgency.

In the *'Wolfsschanze'* the leaders gathered. General Warliamont spoke in his diary of a turnaround in the war to the detriment of Germany; he also included Africa and the increasing aerial bombing of Germany. It was clear that the Russian successes could also have consequences for the southern *Heeresgruppe A*. In the process, new loss figures were also released. Since the start of the offensive until 31.10.1942, Army Group A had lost more than 85,000 troops, more than 11,500 of whom had been killed. Antonescu, the Romanian dictator, offered fresh troops, but given their deplorable equipment, this did not carry any weight. A new ostrich policy began: having first ignored the Soviet buildup of forces in the Volga knee, they now insisted on the heroism of the 6th Army and the coming reinforcements that should bring relief to the trapped troops. In this, an unwarranted optimism resounded. Rokossowski, the Russian supreme commander of the *Don Front*, believed that the Germans had 'miscalculated' and 'the strength and capabilities of the Red Army were underestimated'. Russian resistance was so dogged that even the Russians joked that their 4th Pz.Army under the command of general Krjutschenkin had exactly '4 tanks' left. To supply Stalingrad by air, 298 aircraft were immediately available on the German side, while simple arithmetic showed that 500 were needed. Nevertheless, Hitler let it be known:

'The 6th Army is temporarily surrounded by Russian forces. I intend to assemble the army in the Stalingrad-North area, Kotluban - hill 137 - hill 135 - Marinovka - Zybenko - Stalingrad-South. The army may be assured that I will do everything to supply it sufficiently and relieve it in time. I know the brave 6th Army and itscommander and know that they will do their duty.'

- Hitler.

Friedrich Paulus, the commander of the 6th Army, was certainly dutiful. In many ways, Hitler could not have wished for a more obedient commander. How different the battle of Stalingrad could have been if it had been led by a headstrong commander like Paul Hausser, who at Kharkov in 1943 simply disobeyed the '*Führer*' order to hold his ground, let the Russians into the city and then, in Clausewitz' terms, made them feel 'the flaming sword of retaliation' by throwing the Soviets out frontally and concentrically. Or Herbert Otto Gille, who was ordered to hold out at Stuhlweissenburg, in March 1945, but wihtout the protection of his corps commander (Hermann Breith), simply ignored the order and headed west towards the '*Reichsschutzstellung*'. With Stalin, such behaviour would immediately lead to execution. With Hitler, they sometimes got away with it. Only shortly before Stalingrad, near Kerch, a commander of an infantry division had retreated far, literally giving the Soviets a foothold again. The commander was relieved of his post, given the death penalty, but he was later suspended. It was only when Berlin was already in flames that the SD's flying commandos got hold of him and dealt with him.

Paulus, from good-bourgeois family, had made a *career* under General Walther von Reichenau. This darling of Hitler was everything Paulus was not. Reichenau was loud, brash, *ruthless* when necessary, verging on destructive, but also a man who could make decisions at lightning speed and react spontaneously to things. Paulus, who operated in his shadow, was the man who complemented him in what Von Reichenau lacked; Paulus was controlled, very precise, sensitive and knew the long toes of his superior. This made them a successful duo. Until his death from a heart attack and subsequent plane crash, in January 1942, Von Reichenau was commander of the 6th Army. As much was determined by chance in the history surrounding Stalingrad, Paulus now surfaced, probably partly due to good contacts with Halder. Behind the tall finely honed figure was an unsuspected vanity, and history would initially favour him. Timoshenko's May offensive at Kharkov suddenly made Paulus a famous man. The riveting victory here over the Soviets put Paulus in the spotlight enormously. The '*Ritterkreuz*' followed on 26 May, and the entire German press had his name on its lips. The Third Reich craved new heroes, and Paulus became the hope of the future. His chief of staff was *Oberst* (colonel) Heim and later *Oberst* Schmidt.

The Transience of Fame

Fame is fleeting though, as Paulus too noticed when the Soviets closed in on Stalingrad. There has sometimes been too much of a perception that Paulus was merely a mouthpiece of Hitler and allowed himself to be led unwillingly to the slaughter. This is incorrect. Firstly, Paulus and his staff immediately realised that the position in Stalingrad was unsustainable in the long run and that an adequate air supply was an illusion. Meanwhile, their own forces were too weak to effectively support the collapsing Romanian fronts; in addition, units like General Heim's were also suffering from fuel shortages. On 22 November, Paulus, in consultation with Wolfgang Pickert (9th Flak Div.) and Hoth, concluded that a quick breakout was the best solution. Paulus neither wanted nor dared to take direct action, but wanted to nest in the '*Kessel*' in such a way that a favourable starting position - one thought to the south-west - was possible. Later, Paulus shared his breakout idea with *Heeresgruppe commander* Von Weichs, and on the evening of 23 November 1942 he shared this view with Hitler. '*Bitte Aufgrund der Lage nochmals um Handlungsfreiheit. Heil mein Führer*. Paulus'.

Paulus' biographer Torsten Diedrich writes that at this point Paulus should have followed Erwin Rommel's example in Africa, turned off the radio and broken out. Everyone would have been faced with a *fait accompli*, the Germans could have pulled back on the Don and at least saved many lives, including at *Heeresgruppe A*.

Operation 'Wintergewitter'

Construction of Soviet tank ditch

But Paulus did not, and so he ended up handing himself over to Hitler who, along with Jodl, and supported by *Luftwaffe* boss Hermann Göring, was in favour of retaining the city. Internally, Paulus was now also under pressure. General Walther von Seydlitz-Kurzbach already withdrew troops on his own initiative, but when the breakout failed to materialise, this led to unpleasant position disputes in which General Georg Pfeiffer's 94th Inf.Div. suffered heavy losses. Von Seydlitz-Kurzbach did not let this throw him off course and submitted a '*Denkschrift*' the next day, arguing that not breaking out was tantamount to the downfall of the 6th Army. Paulus was dismayed by his general's unresponsiveness, but forwarded the *Denkschrift*, which was right up his street, to the *Heeresgruppe*. However, no real decision was made. General Erwin Jaenecke of the IV Army Corps, in retrospect, believed that Paulus, 'despite all his cleverness, was too weak to resist Hitler', and that he 'feared Hitler's wrath more than the Red Army's sword of Damocles'.

Still, there were also practical concerns why Paulus could not break out immediately. The 6th Army was still in combat, thus needed outside support and this had to be coordinated at a high level first, while outside the '*Kessel*' it was a huge chaos with the collapsing Romanian Armies and the later follow-up attacks against the Italians and Hungarians. If things went wrong, not only the troops from Stalingrad were at stake, but the entire *Heeresgruppe*, and this in turn had consequences for *Heeresgruppe A* in the Caucasus, which could be cut off. Here the losses during the campaign and the lack of combat-ready strategic reserves began to take their revenge. In doing so, Paulus was a military man who realised that this was also a political decision, and earlier Hitler had saved the front with his 'halting order' in winter 1941-1942. Hitler had often had martial luck on his side until Stalingrad, and this had brought him *prestige*. Von Manstein confirmed this in his memoirs. According to him, Hitler had drawn the conclusion from the winter of 1941-1942 that much could be gained with willpower and obstinacy. In itself, Hitler was right that holding out (defending) was the strongest form of combat if one had air superiority, but of course this was not independent of a good supply and the presence of internal transport capacities and supply lines. That was no longer the case at Stalingrad.

Finally, there was disagreement within their own ranks: Seydlitz preferred to break out immediately while the ring still had weaknesses, Schmidt was obedient to Hitler. Paulus was stuck and did not have the weight to form a broad internal front and push through. This left the initiative in the hands of the Red Army that would reduce the *Kessel* step by step, and on outside help, which eventually came.

'Wintergewitter' - Panzer Raid to Stalingrad, the Failed Disengagement Attempt

The German disengagement offensive fell to the successfull conqueror of Sebastopol, Von Manstein. On 28 November, he had been appointed the new *Heeresgruppe commander* Don. Although the army group consisted of six armies, Hitler, as always, wanted to hold on to everything that had been achieved. This left the *overstretch in place*, which left Von Manstein with only two armoured divisions to be freed to relieve Stalingrad with.

The Kotelnikowo railway junction was the most logical and eastern starting point for a *panzer raid* to Stalingrad. It had the advantage of being a familiar route for *Armeegruppe Hoth* (*LVII. Pz.Corps: General der Panzertruppe* Friedrich Kirchner). The 4th Pz.Army had taken the same route towards Rokotino some weeks before. The disadvantage was that the waterways were at right angles to it and could not always be avoided: Aksaj, Mischkowa, the small Mischkowa and the Donskaya Zariza. The showpiece of the disengagement offensive was General Raus' 6th Pz.Div. This unit from Wuppertal was in excellent condition, with 160 tanks and 40 *Sturmgeschütze*. The other available 23rd Pz.Div. (recalled from the Caucasus) was a full division only on paper and had only 30 tanks. Very worrying, actually, unacceptable and against any military logic, was the lack of infantry such as motorised infantry divisions. With some distance, Romanian infantry would follow, though, and troopers from the 17th Pz.Div. from the Orel area, commanded by General Frido von Senger und Etterlin.

'*Wintergewitter*' was christened the operation, which started on 12 December. Initially, Kirchner achieved success. The Soviet lines were broken through. 150 kilometres had to be covered. The Russian Marshal Zhukov, who had become increasingly responsible for the action around Stalingrad, had expected the German attack. Lines had been built up to repel an attack, but the relatively early start of the attack nevertheless surprised the Soviets. Still, much went wrong immediately. The main attack force, *Gruppe Hühnersdorff (Pz.Rgt. 11)*, started an hour late. Due to traffic chaos in Kotelnikowo, they were stuck for some time, while the other assault groups, the armoured grenadier regiments of the 6th Pz.Division (114 under Zollenkopf and 4 under Unrein) were already on the attack. As it was already getting dark at 3.30pm, every hour counted. On the east flank the 23rd Pz.Div. entered, and later the 17th Pz.Div. would follow on the west flank. After the slow start, *Gruppe Hühnersdorff advanced* towards Gremjatschij, which was captured together with Romanian infantry at 06:45. In order not to lose time, they refuelled in the open field and continued towards Tschilekoff. This place was on the railway line and formed a fast road to the Aksaj river and to Wassiljewka, on the Mischkowa river, where a second bridgehead was to be formed. But a curious thing happened. While the first signs pointed to a total surprise on the Russian side, they nevertheless opted for a very cautious tactic. *Gruppe* Hühnersdorff did not push further in a north-easterly direction, but turned away from the railway to the west, towards the town of Werchne Jablotschnij, which was attacked by *Pz.Gren Rgt. 4* (Unrein). Where the motto of German tank expert Heinz Guderian had always been 'drive on, do not muddle through', here, flank cover took priority over exploiting the surprise effect. The 'attack' westward through Hühnersdorff was a completely unnecessay *manoeuvre*. The road to Werchne Jablotschnij was difficult to traverse, and when the tanks finally arrived, Unrein had long since taken the place without meeting much resistance. After this miraculous battle in the air, Hühnersdorff had to turn right, take the difficult road again, to continue northwards again. When Hühnersdorff arrived at Tschilekoff, it appeared that here, too, the work had already been done. The reconnaissance department of the 6th Pz.Div. under Quentin, had already taken the place. Here, too, the Red army had offered only minor resistance. General Raus realised that *momentum* was in danger of being lost, and urged Hühnersdorff to make up for lost time and penetrate to the Aksaj still during the night. But it was already dark early and Hühnersdorff successfully resisted the order. The tanks of the 6th Pz.Div. remained where they stood.

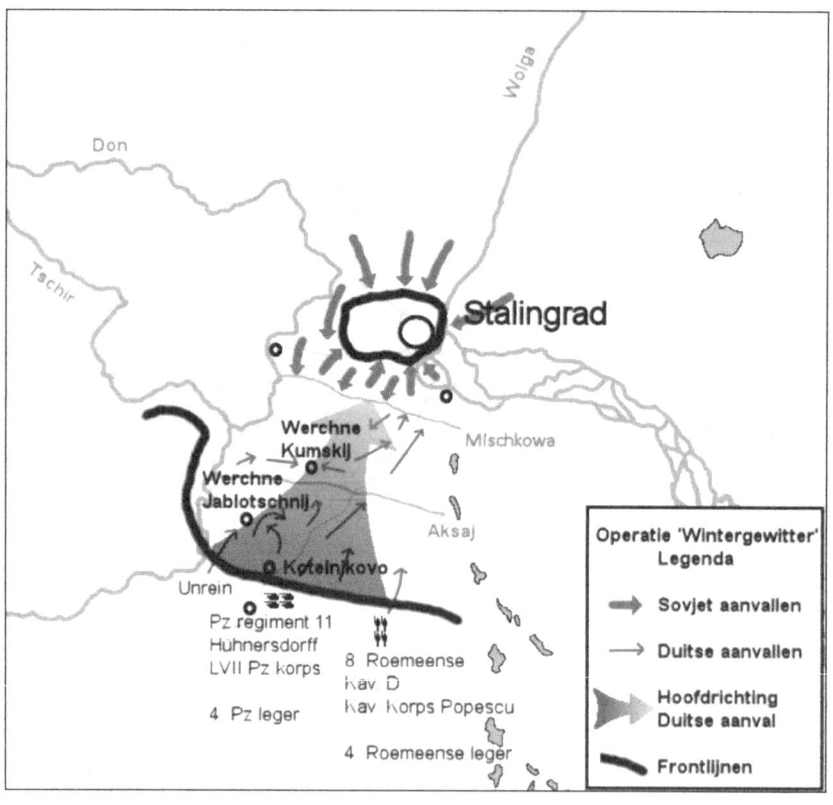

Oberst Walter Von Hühnersdorff, Commander of the Pz. Rgt. 11 (6. Pz. D)

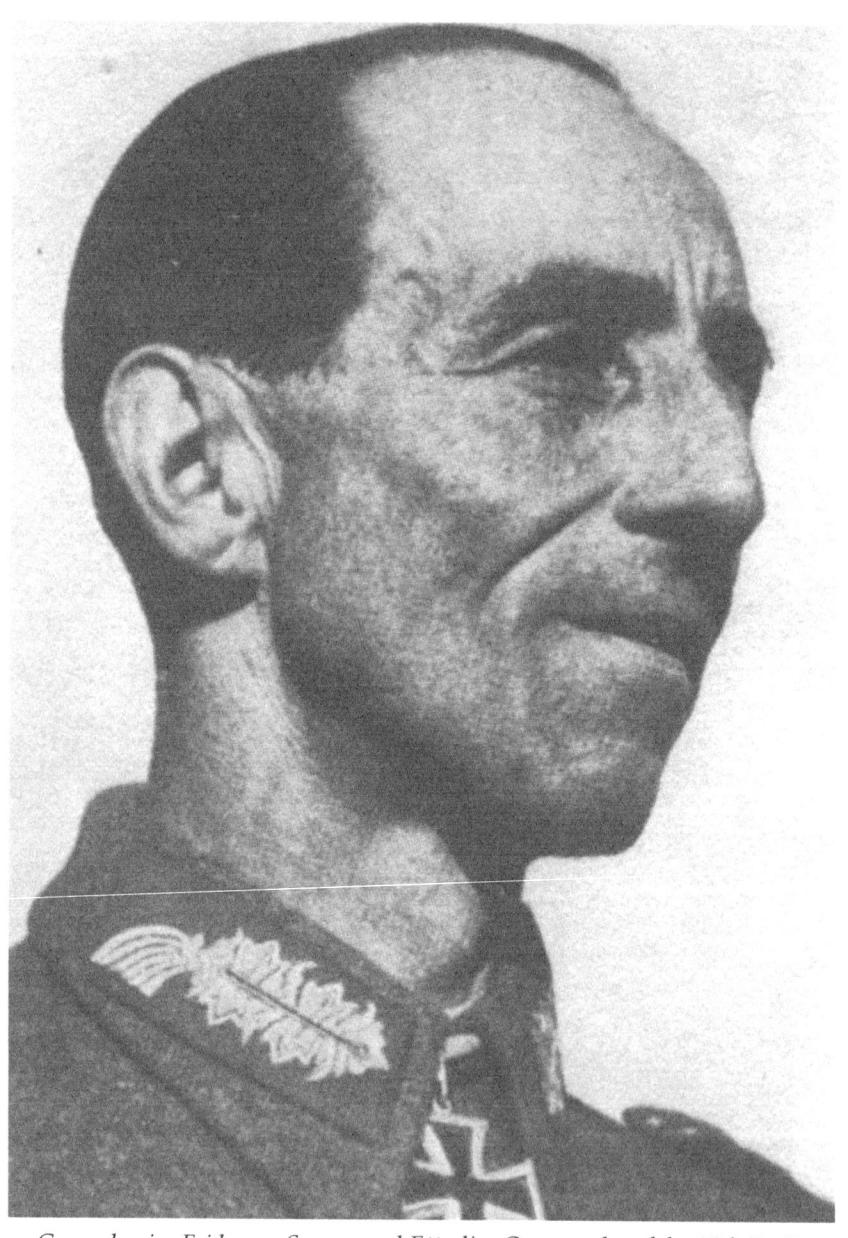

Generalmajor Frido von Senger und Etterlin, Commander of the 17th Pz. D

Bridgehead Aksaj

An almost surreal picture emerged. The core force of '*Win- tergewitter*', the 6th Pz.Div., had not suffered one casualty on the first day of attack, covered many laborious unnecessary kilometres and the first objective, a bridgehead across the Aksaj, had not been achieved. We can only guess at the explanation. In any case, it seemed that the German units no longer operated with the élan and naturalness as before. Hühnersdorff apparently felt vulnerable on the flanks without sufficient infantry support - did not trust the Russian defection - and therefore pursued its own zigzag course to avoid surprises. A sign, that obtaining or disseminating combat intelligence was no longer working properly. Air intelligence should have reassured or warned the troop commanders of flank attacks.

The very next day, Quentin's reconnaissance division noticed rapidly growing Soviet resistance. The Red Army had been awakened and was trying to prevent a further advance towards Stalingrad. On 13 December, Quentin reported the first Soviet tanks; they were units of the Red Army's 4th and 13th Mechanised Brigades, which together with the 4th Guards Cav.Corps, the 126th and 302 Russian I.D. were the 51st Army's main units in the area. Quentin had to call on *Pz.Rgt. 11* from Hühnersdorff. This seemed to have understood the lesson of the previous day, headed due north and established a bridgehead across the Aksaj at Saliwsky. The next intermediate stop to Mischkowa was supposed to be Werchne Kumskij. But fate decided otherwise. As Von Hühnersdorff's command tank drove over the bridge at Aksaj, it collapsed. The heavy tank remained stuck. People tried feverishly to pull it away, but it was stuck. There was no other option but to build a new bridge.

To save time, Raus urged Hühnersdorff, with the tanks already present in the bridgehead (*1./ Pz.Rgt.11*), to continue the offensive. There were no artillery and grenadiers. Hühnersdorff fell back on his cautious approach as a result. No sooner was the town attacked than air support arrived. Only after the *Stuka bombardment* did they attack. At noon, Werchne Kumsky was in German hands. Again, there was hardly any Russian resistance and precious time had been wasted. There is even the question of whether air support had been necessary. Meanwhile, the reconnaissance division was getting into more and more trouble and parts of *Pz.Rgt 11* - now with good reason - had to come to the aid of the flanks. This flank threat would remain a festering wound in the side of Raus' corps. After the capture of Werchne Kumsky, the *LVII. Pz.Corps* still acted hesitantly. The temperature was getting colder and colder and there was no solid front, which could not be done without proper infantry support. The men were increasingly fearful of being surrounded themselves, knowing what had happened at Stalingrad and Hitler's reaction. Meanwhile, the 23rd Pz.Div. was also on the Aksaj and had formed a small bridgehead on the north bank. It was decided not to drive northwards unilaterally, but to opt for consolidation first. In defence of Raus, Hühnersdorff and Kirchner, it must be stated that Hitler was very intransigent about the necessary freedom of movement for Paulus in Stalingrad. Instead of allowing it to move towards the *LVII. Pz.Corps* to fight, nothing happened. A narrow passage as a 'lock' or corridor was therefore not enough, given the distance. Only a 'wide' free-fighting of Stalingrad would really make any difference within this fact.

Time played in the Red Army's favour. Between 14 and 17 December, more and more tank battles developed in the area of the *LVII. Pz.Corps*. At breakneck speed, units of the 2nd Guards Army, commanded by General Malinovsky, and General Popov's 5th Thrust Army, moved to the 'Kotelnikowo sector', as the Soviets called this front section. In these battles, Hühnersdorff still achieved notable successes, such as a surprise attack on gathering Soviet tanks, destroying 34 *T-34* tanks, but German fighting strength was also noticeably dwindling. Meanwhile, the Soviets led the 234th Pz.Rgt. and a tank destruction brigade, with plenty of anti-tank artillery. Without generous infantry support, these units were do- dable to the German assault force. On 15 December, the battle north of Werchne Kumsky was mainly characterised by un-supervised tank battles in all directions. The Soviets now had anti-tank artillery linked behind their tanks, which successfully engaged the Germans on the battlefield. Hühnersdorff had to deploy fog grenades to hide the German units from view, destroying the *Pak*. As the battle slowly unfolded in German favour, von Hühnersdorff received bad news from Werchne Kumskij. The small garrison that had remained in the town was in danger of being rolled up by the Red Army. *Pz.Rgt. 11* turned right around and rolled towards its own troops. They were just in time to evacuate the remaining garrison commanded by Major Löwe. Hühnersdorff decided to clear the place and fall back to the bridgehead at Saliwskij.

Hopes were now pinned on the 17th Pz.Div. According to divisional commander Frido von Senger und Etterlin, this unit was cut from 'the right cloth'. Only the officer corps, partly stemming from World War I, sometimes had some old-fashioned ideas. However, the division had a good reputation and Hoth insisted that 'the Stalingrad case had to be solved'. Yet the 17th was far from full strength and had left Orel in such haste that repair units had not even come along. On 18 December, the 17th Pz.Div. established a bridgehead across the Aksaj near Generalowskij, while the Red Army concentrated on Saliwskij and Werchne Kumskij. It was the *Rgt. 63*, the '*Gruppe Seitz*', which was the first to cross the river. On the advance to the north, however, the 17th Pz.Div. encountered dogged Soviet resistance at the *kolkhoz* '8 March'. After an hour-long tank duel, the position was taken by Von Senger und Etterlin. Fifteen *T-34s* dug in to the turret were destroyed in the process. The gain in terrain allowed the 17th Pz.Div. and the 6th Pz.Div. to act concentrically against the Soviet defenders, so that units under Diasamidse's command in and around Werchne Kumskij were in danger of being encircled and broke out to the north. Once again, Werchne Kumskij was in German hands.

The 17th Pz.Div. immediately took advantage of this and advanced towards the Myschowka river. The division commander personally took command at the spearhead. For a brief moment there seemed to be hope again for a success of *'Wintergewitter'*. But on 20 December 1942, the curtain finally fell on the operation. Bitter street fighting unfolded in Nish Kumsky and the development of a major bridgehead failed to materialise. The Soviet marine soldier Ilya Kaplunow made history here by destroying no German tanks all by himself. His comrades found his body by following his blood trail among the burning tank carcasses.

Hoth and Raus were still trying their luck further east. A small bridgehead was established, but each subsequent step forward presented a new problem in the flank. The *momentum* was over and sufficient infantry support was not there. Commander Seitz of *Rgt. 63* died. The *17. Pz.Div.* was now in the same position as the 23rd and 6th Pz.Div. earlier. One had to defend all sides.

Von Manstein was now reaching for a last resort. His head of military intelligence, Major Eismann, had been flown in to Stalingrad to consult with Paulus. Von Manstein also sounded out the OKH. Operation *'Wintergewitter'* was to be followed by operation *'Donnerschlag'*, the breakout of the 6th Army from Stalingrad towards the Kotelnikowo group. Paulus listed all the objections to this operation and then quoted the *Füher order*. On 21 December, Von Manstein telegraphed Hitler himself in extreme vertigo. But here he heard the same arguments. The 6th Army had to stay where it was.

In ten days, the *LVII. Pz.Corps* had advanced eighty kilometres. At the northernmost position, they were at one point 48 kilometres from Stalingrad. In the meantime, the 6th Pz.Div. had lost 1,100 men, and had only a fraction of its equipment. It was clear that destruction was imminent for the *LVII. Pz.Corps* if it stood its ground so far forward. Retreat was inevitable.

On 20 December 1942, the order for the retreat came in. On 22 December, Malinovsky noted that the Red Army had taken over the initiative. The German assault force was now pursuing itself.

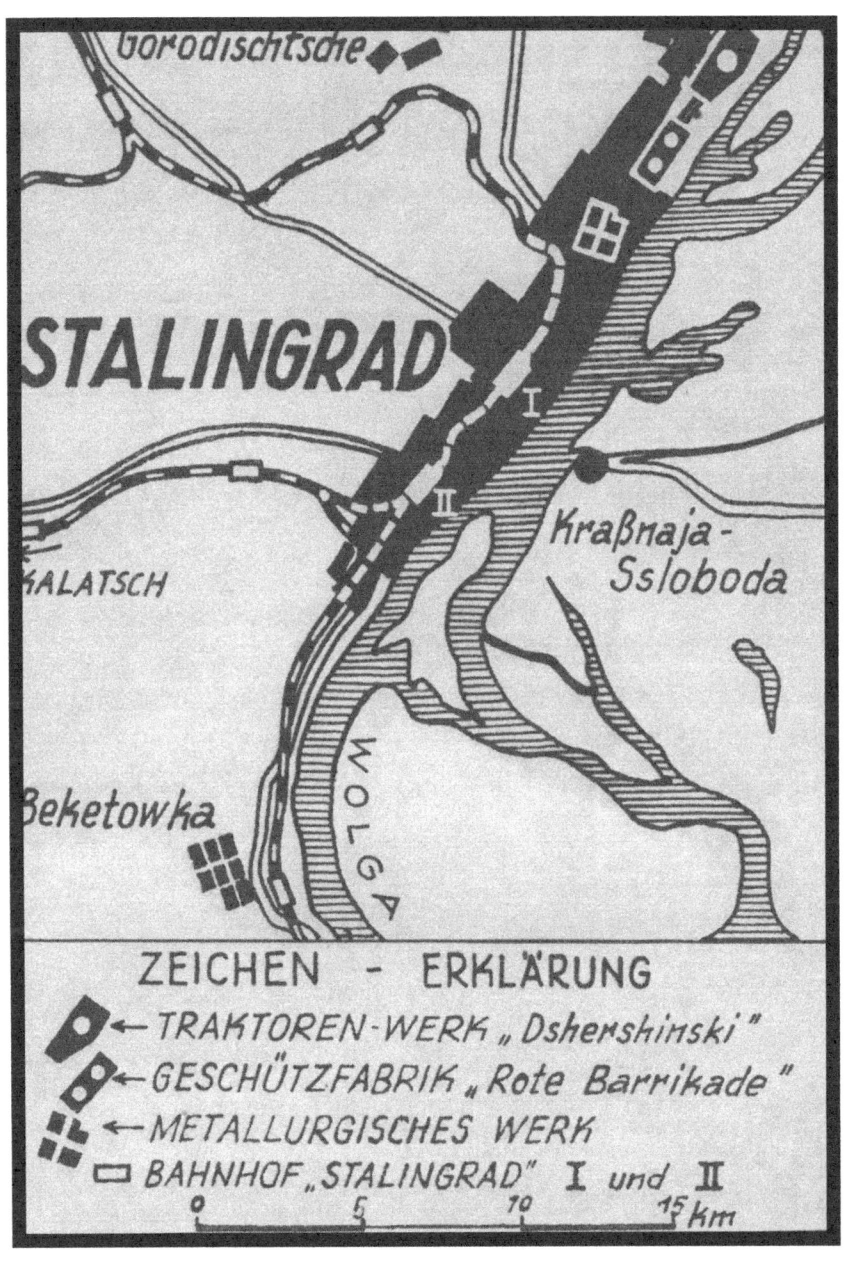

Strategic positions Stalingrad

PzKw. IV, Stalingrad

Don at Kalatsch

Soviet infantry man Stalingrad

Photos above and below, 21 August 1942, the crossing of the Don

Stalingrad

Armoured infantry, Stalingrad

Street view Stalingrad

Ju 52 transport aircraft

General Paulus and his adjutant Wilhelm Adam

Ra/381/2530/2.7.

Fernschreibstelle Odysseus II 104

4L 3 5 5 13

Fernschreibname Laufende Nr.

Angenommen
Aufgenommen

Datum: 2/7 1942

um: 2055 Uhr

von: HLG X

durch:

Befördert:

Datum: 19

um: Uhr

an:

durch:

Rolle:

Vermerke:

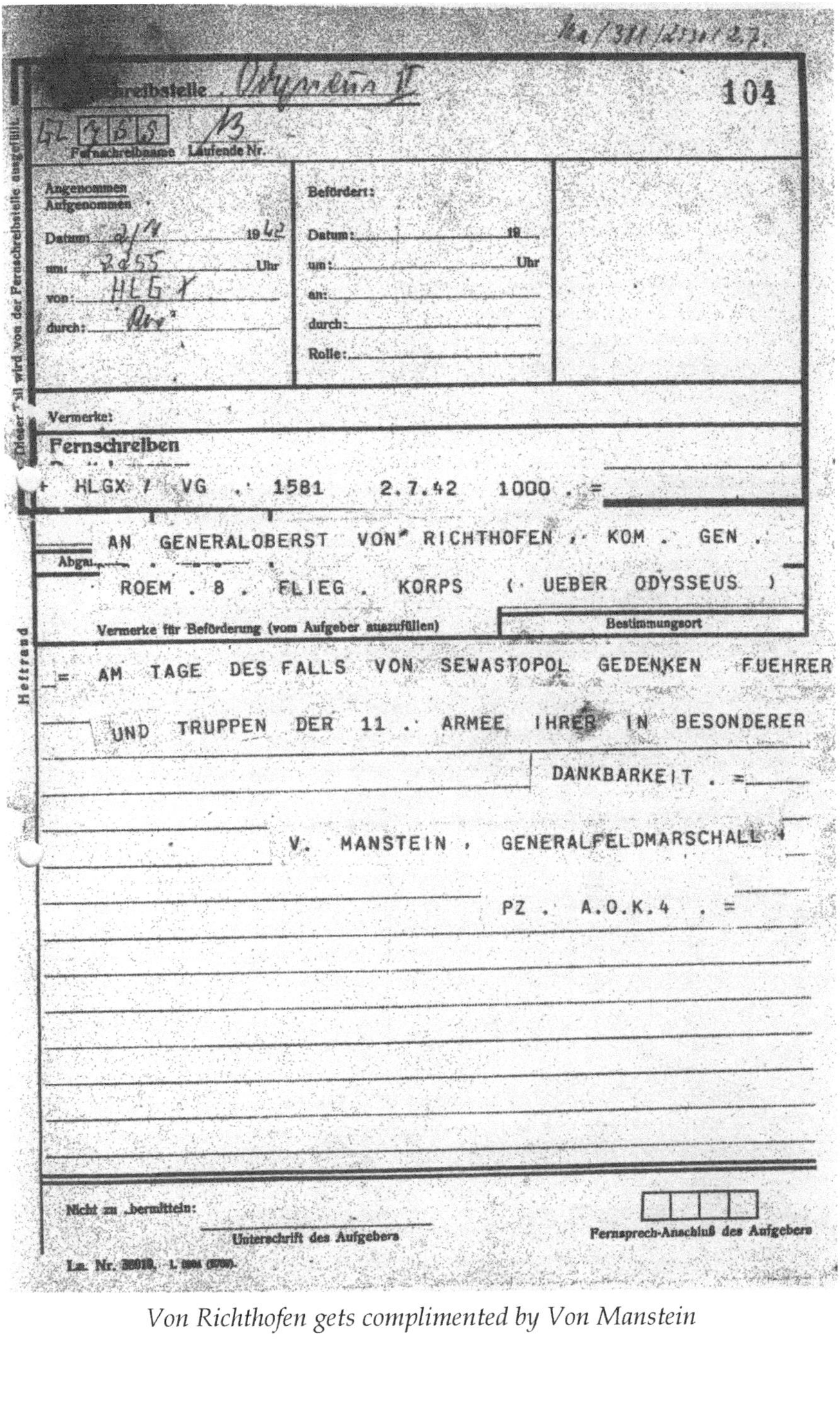

Fernschreiben

\+ HLGX / VG . 1581 2.7.42 1000 . =

AN GENERALOBERST VON RICHTHOFEN , KOM . GEN .

Abgang

ROEM . 8 . FLIEG . KORPS (UEBER ODYSSEUS)

Vermerke für Beförderung (vom Aufgeber auszufüllen) Bestimmungsort

= AM TAGE DES FALLS VON SEWASTOPOL GEDENKEN FUEHRER UND TRUPPEN DER 11 . ARMEE IHRER IN BESONDERER DANKBARKEIT . =

V. MANSTEIN , GENERALFELDMARSCHALL

PZ . A.O.K.4 . =

Nicht zu übermitteln:

Unterschrift des Aufgebers

Fernsprech-Anschluß des Aufgebers

Heftrand

Dieser Teil wird von der Fernschreibstelle ausgefüllt

Von Richthofen gets complimented by Von Manstein

- 488 -

21.8.1942

5.30 los zum LI.A.K.(Gen.v.Seidlitz), das im Norden am rechten Flügel neuen Brückenkopf für Panzerdurchbruch macht. Erst zur Aufklärungsgruppe am Nordbogen Don. Dann auf Beobachtungs- und Gefechtsstand des Korps mit sehr guter Übersicht. Ruhiger Betrieb. Rechts sehr gut vor, links erst hängen bleiben und dann vor. Feind viel schwächer als erwartet; wird vom Heer stets überschätzt; ist fertig; eigene Panzer und Infanterie aber wenig leistungsfähig. - Weiter zu XIV.A.K.(Gen.v.Wietersheim bedenklich wie stets, aber zuversichtlich, nur langsam. - Dort auch Kdr. VIII.A.K.(alten Bekannten Heitz) getroffen. Weiter zu 389. und 384.J.Div. (Gen.Jaenicke und Gen. Frhr.v.Gablentz) zuversichtlich, aber schwach. - Nachmittags erweiterten sie ihre Brückenköpfe planmässig; auch bei LI.A.K.wurden die Voraussetzungen für die Brücken geschaffen und eine bereits gebaut. - In der Luft anfangs wenig los, im Laufe des Tages aber doch 44 Abschüsse. - Über Schlachtfeld Kalatsch zurück. Unglaublich viele rote Panzer und Tote. - Zu Hitschold (Schlächter), der wie stets frisch, lustig und munter. Sehr guter Mann! - Nach Hause, d.h. ins Zeltlager. Flog über teils bebaute, meist/ganz kahle, stark wellige, trostlose Steppe.- Bei Jaenickes Division als Nafü Hansi Studnitz (frisch, mager und dankbar); die "Flucht an die Front".- Regiert, Papier, Zukunft. -

4.Pz. nur mit rechtem Flügel etwas vor. Schlappheit. IV.A.K. blieb völlig liegen bezw. trat garnicht an. - Russen brachten 150 km ostw. Stalingrad zwei Divisionen über die Wolga; wurden von K.G.76 2 x gehascht. "Blut gerührt"! Wehrten sich nicht und schossen garnicht wieder. Scheinbar ganz unausgebildete Leute. -

22.8.1942

Aufklärungskdre. Konflikt mit Uebe. - Von 10.00 - 15.00 auf K-Plätzen; etwas geölt. Zu Hause(Zeltlager) regiert. Oberst Harlinghausen, Befehl für morgigen Großtag stark beeinflusst. in Torpedofragen Kdre. auch von mir aus noch gespritzt. Wenn Heer einigermassen mitmacht, muss es morgen klar gehen. -

Heute leidliches Vorkommen im Südraum. Keine grosse Sache und noch weniger Willen, daher nur halbe Einsätze.- Italiener

-489-

War diary of Von Richthofen about the front at Kalatsch

Paulus, commander of the 6th Army. Photo from 1941

Paulus

March of the 4th Pz. Army

The burning suburbs of Stalingrad

German soldiers with a MG 34 in the Kalmückensteppe, with a disabled Soviet tank in the background

Newspaper 17 September 1942

German artillery, Stalingrad

MG-stellung

Wounded Germans at a Ju 52

Ju 52 – Stalingrad

Photo from 12 January 1943 at a runover position of the XIV Pz. Corps

'Einzelkämpfer'

*Glorification of German soldier, from the
'Völkischer Beobachter' 04-02-1943*

Fallen Soviet soldier

Stuka's above Stalingrad

Stalingrad

Generalmajor Schmidt

Gift from 'the Führer'

Soviet prisoners of war

German troops retreat to the city

Joseph Goebbels – Nazi Minister of Propaganda

Bizarre photo: Soviet T-34 tank and German Ju 87 aircraft lie next to each other on the battlefield

Hermann Göring, commander of the German 'Luftwaffe'

The *Madonna* of Stalingrad and the Retreat from Caucasus

This is how Christmas fell in Stalingrad. Symbolic of the terrible suffering was the doctor Kurt Reuter's drawing of the '*Madonna* of Stalingrad'. This poignant charcoal drawing expressed the lost feelings of many. The doctor did not survive the hell of Stalingrad; the drawing was flown out.

On 8 January, the Russians demanded the surrender of the Germans at Stalingrad. Paulus again asked for freedom of action, but Hitler remained insensitive to the request. There were always reasons to keep obeying anyway. On 28 December, they had finally begun to take back *Heeresgruppe A* from the Caucasus. This was a complex undertaking that was laborious. About 200,000 men, 7,000 artillery pieces and 300 tanks had to be moved in a north-westerly direction. A collapse of Stalingrad, followed by a Russian thrust on Rostov, would be an unprecedented disaster.

Due to the enormous debacle at Stalingrad, this equally dramatic period on the Eastern Front, both for the German and Russian sides, has always remained somewhat forgotten. This is mainly because this was a colossal (logistical) undertaking, full of human suffering. Hardly mentioned in the literature is the fact that German troops literally died here from malnutrition and exhaustion, for example, due to the endless *speed marches*, poor nutrition and fighting under harsh conditions. Especially the young, inexperienced soldiers died from this. Dr Buchka, divisional doctor of the 97th *Jäger-Division*, wrote on 6.12.1942: '*The nutritional situation is catastrophic. The patholo-*

Madonna of Stalingrad

gist-anatomist has confirmed this on the basis of inspection of soldiers who died of exhaustion. Many soldiers have lost considerable weight (without any fat) and barely possess reserves. In practice, every second or third man in the field is sick: bronchitis, diarrhoea, rheumatism. Many suffer forms of heart damage from exhaustion. As a result of the continuous actions, the eternally wet weather and the almost hopeless situation, a far-reaching apathy and indifference of the people towards their state of health and the need for cleanliness and hygiene has arisen, especially in the Jäger companies [...] In addition, there is a huge lice problem that cannot be combated with medicines (Russla powder) alone, under these unfavourable living conditions. This has led to hefty skin infections. [...] In general, we can say that the state of health is in a highly questionable situation. [...] The division needs rest and better care. Since October and the beginning of the re- time, the situation has deteriorated dramatically. The following cases occurred in the front lines and in the field hospital: 12 dead from heart failure and exhaustion, 4 died from kidney poisoning, 2 died from jaundice and exhaustion, 2 men drowned and 1 died from carbon monoxide poisoning.

Dr Buchka advocated the establishment of a proper delousing facility at the new field hospital at Gunaika. He also advocated making the best use of the existing hospitals (at Chadishenskaya, among others) and ensuring that soldiers were given new clean clothes, especially socks, and good leather grease to work the boots with and keep dry feet. In spite of this divisional doctor's efforts, the losses of the *97. Jäger-Div.* was rapidly mounting. A total overview showed that since the Russia Field Campaign until 31 December 1942, this division had already suffered 2491 casualties, including 78 officers. The number of wounded was astronomical, with 10,502 troops and 302 officers. To this was added just under 200 missing. To sum up, total losses, including wounded, were over 13,000 men and non-commissioned officers (practically an entire division) and about 400 officers. This was no exception; the 125th I.D., for example, also part of the *XXXXIV.Corps*, lost 10,461 men to dead, wounded and missing in the same period, 2081 of whom were fallen men and non-commissioned officers, and 83 officers; the *101.Jäger-Div.* lost 10,990 men and non-commissioned officers, of which 2372 were killed, and 72 officers.

Mountain Corps General Konrad (*XXXXIX. Geb.ArmeeKorps*) still tried to give his troops a cheer on 1 January 1943: *'Sieg heil den Divisionen und anderen Einheiten des Gebirgs-Armeekorps im Neuen Jahr',* he opened his New Year's wish, then went on to state: '*Und wenn die Welt voll Teufel wär, es wird uns doch gelingen!*' He spoke of the 'divine duty' to fight for *Grossdeutschland* and Europe, closing with *'Sieg heil Kameraden im Neuen Jahr!'* Corps commander Hermann Breith's private diary paints a considerably more sober picture.

12 January 1943: visit to 370th Inf. Division exhausted. Bad weather, with impassable roads.
14 January 1943: Very cold.
15 January 1943: New positions *13. Pz.Div*. visited. Cold east wind, very cold.
17 January 1943: We are breathless. Difficult connections with 370th Inf.Div. Very severe lack of arms and equipment, especially with *Inf.Rgt. 667.*
21 January 1943: accelerated retreat necessary.
22 January 1943: visit to 370th I.D. as it leaves the corps.
23 January 1943: Strong snowfall. Bottomless roads.
28 January 1943: Very cold, visit to *Pz.A.O.K.4*
31 January 1943: visit to *Heeresgruppe*, not very encouraging.
3 February 1943: very serious situation, especially with the 19th Pz.Division.

And so it went on.

In the book *Blutiges Edelweiss,* historian Hermann Frank Meyer described the history of the *1.GebirgsDivision*. It was the unit that, among other things, raised the Nazi flag on the summit of the Elbrus; renamed the 'Adolf Hitler summit'. Hitler, incidentally, was furious about this; he saw it as vanity that distracted from his much desired breakthrough to the Black Sea and to the Afrika Korps. Meyer outlines the particularly bloody battles of the XXXXIX General Konrad's mountain corps through the Mountain Caucasus, during which the division, together with sister division *4. Geb.Div.*, fought its way south through the mountains for 200 kilometres. Starting at the Kuban River (August), they advanced through the Tebera Valley and the Kluchor Pass, until the Red Army stopped the advance at the end of August. They then tried again to move south through the Forest Caucasus and Maikop. On 21 October, they stood exhausted before the Semanskhoberg, the last natural obstacle before the Black Sea. The supply lines had become so long that troops were starving. Some units kept themselves alive with chestnuts found on the ground.

The ambitious division commander of the *1. Geb.Div.*, Hubert Lanz, drove his troops *ruthlessly into* battle. The mountain was eventually captured, but could not be held. The Soviets constantly brought in reinforcements. On 12 December 1942, Hitler authorised the retreat. In just 17 days, the *1. Geb.Div.* left another 456 killed, 1443 wounded and 187 missing. No fewer than 4250 horses lost their lives. Since the start of Operation *'Barbarossa',* the division had suffered losses of 18,025 men, out of a total strength of 19,437. Lanz was awarded the *Ritterkreuz* by Hitler, but command of the division passed to General Walter Karl Hugo Stettner *Ritter* von Grabenhofen, the former commander of the *Gebirgsjäger Rgt. 99* during the Norway Field Mission.

Disastrous for the Red Army and the civilian population was the very large-scale destruction carried out by the Germans during their retreat from the Caucasus. The Freiburg archives contain many reports, mostly from the various pioneer battalions (*Pi. Btl. 9, 97, 46, 101* and *Eisenbahn* pioneer units - *Regiment 3*, streamlined by the *Korpspionierführer* of the XXXXIV Army Corps -Pi.*Rgts.Stab 673*), on the destruction that went from airfields (e.g. *Krimskaya* airfield) to bridges (dozens, such as bridges in the Krimskaja- Kiewskoje route) to dairies and leather farms.

On 10 January, the Russians reopened the offensive on Stalingrad. Especially from the west, they succeeded in pressing the area, two-thirds of the terrain in and around the city was lost. Especially serious was the loss of airfields that followed in the following weeks: as *Basargino* (south-west), *Pitomnek* (west) and *Gumrak* (closest to the city-west). The situation was now deteriorating rapidly. Despite all the promises of Hitler and Göring, only 31% of the promised supplies arrived between 10 and 17 January 1943.

Meanwhile, the 6th Army was in danger of starving and Paulus ordered the Russian prisoners of war that had been gathered at Woroponowo southwest of Stalingrad - in the area of the *297. Inf.Div.* - be released.

Hitler's response to the distress were promotions and sub- promotions; the *Ritterkreuz* for Schmidt and the *Eichenlaub* for Paulus. As a last-ditch attempt, Paulus had *Hauptmann* Winrich Behr flown out via *Gumrak*. Via Von Manstein's main quarters in Tagangrog, Behr managed to penetrate the '*Wolfsschanze*' where, at Paulus's behest, he had to present Hitler with the disastrous situation of the 6th Army in no uncertain terms. As always, Hitler again conjured a few promises of hope out of the hat, three *Waffen SS* divisions would come to liberate Stalingrad and until then they had to persevere. He also waved away tales of hunger. In December, Hitler claimed, the 6th Army had also reported having food for another three days, but the army still existed.

The visit was not entirely without consequences. The next day, Behr was again summoned to Hitler, who presented him with new plans made with Air Marshal Erhard Milch to improve the airlift. A new *idée fixe* was in place. Behr travelled on to Paul's wife, a Romanian beauty, whom he personally handed a letter and envelope from Paul. The envelope contained the wedding ring. A better proof of Paul's belief in the further downfall, could hardly be imagined. Behr did not return to the '*Kessel*' again. According to historian Torsten Diedrich, Behr had so clearly demonstrated the truth that Hitler believed Behr would be bad for the morale of the 6th Army. After Behr, Paulus tried again with General Jaenecke. The latter had been wounded in the head. It was not too serious, but Paulus hoped that Jaenecke could convey the 6th Army's views to the OKW. Indeed, on 26 January it came to a meeting with Hitler. The latter shifted the blame to Göring and brought up the new 'plan Milch'.

Meanwhile in Stalingrad, even Paulus' headquarters had to move. Initially located at *Gumrak* airfield, it was moved around 19 - 20 January 1943 to a *balka* on the outskirts of the city, where the 71st Inf.Div. (General Alexander von Hartmann) had its headquarters. They could not hold out for long there either, and eventually the 6th Army staff ended up in the cellars of the *Univermag* department store in the city centre.

The 'Organised Die-off' has Begun

By then, the situation had become dramatic. *Gumrak* airfield had fallen on 22 January, the following day the emergency *Stalingradski* airfield. Supplies could now only be dropped from the air. It was absolutely insufficient. 'The organised die-off has begun,' mused General Hube. The 57th Russian Army had broken through to the city from the southwest. Von Manstein now phoned Hitler himself and asked if Paulus could start surrender negotiations. According to Hitler, this was impossible simply because of 'honour'. Paulus took on this prestige and informed his men on 22 January that he would 'not budge an inch'. According to biographer Diedrich, Schmidt, in particular, was speaking here, but the final responsibility, of course, remained with Paulus. 12,000 wounded lay untended in the city. By 26 January, this number had risen to more than 20,000. Two days later the order was given that the wounded and sick would no longer receive provisions, which were only meant for the fighting troops. Seydlitz made a renewed appeal to Paulus to do something. On 31 January, Hitler promoted Paulus to field marshal. No Prussian marshal had ever surrendered since the Napoleonic Wars, so it could be understood as a silent hint from *Führer headquarters*. Meanwhile, the staff in *Univermag* had decided that it was 'the duty' of the generals to share the fate of the soldiers; so this meant imprisonment. On 29 January, after the *Kessel* had broken up into three parts, Paulus had authorised his officers to make plans on their own.

General Von Hartmann committed suicide, Richard Stempel, the commander of the 371st Inf.Division, sought death on the 'battlefield'. *Generalleutnant* Schlömer of the *XIV. Pz.Korps* tried to start capitulation consultations on his own authority. Small groups, for example commanded by officers Elchepp and Von Kunowksi, tried to break out. The *Univermag* department store was surrounded by the Red Army on the last day of January and telephone lines were cut. Paulus only had control of his closest surroundings and even that he had now given up. The finely- tuned Paulus was not up to the situation, feeling trapped after being promoted by Hitler, and had declared himself a 'private' and placed the leadership of the 'North *Kessel'* in the hands of corps commander (*XI. Corps*) general Strecker, while in the 'south-*Kessel'* the leadership was placed in the hands of general Roske of the 71st Inf.Div. This decision by Paulus is also said to have been prompted by the fact that Goebbels and Göring, both in their speech of 30 January, had not mentioned Paulus at all.

Paul's right-hand man, General Adam, had then come into contact with the 64th Soviet Army and started consultations with General M.S.Schumilov and officers O.A.Vinokur and F.M.Ilyenko of its staff. The latter now negotiated further with Schmidt and Adam. Schmidt finally brought the negotiating boots to Paulus himself, who, very emaciated and with his face full of nerves, received the Russians. He was allowed to keep his chief of staff Adam with him, as well as his personal belongings. Roske and Schmidt had already negotiated that they 'would not kill him' and that the interrogations would be allowed to take place only by 'Rokossovsky'. The fear about Paul's person possibly stemmed from Paul's harsh action against partisans in the Stalingrad area, who would have been executed. Leonid Reschin's book mentioned this issue, which otherwise remained unknown in the Stalingrad literature. Nor would Paulus be held responsible for any independent German action elsewhere after surrender. *So wie so* Paulus no longer had any control over the 'north *Kessel*'. Paulus was a broken man, full of guilt over the downfall of his army. He remained vain though; even in Russian captivity he had the shoulder epaulettes of marshal sent to him by post over neutral lines.

Karl Strecker in the north *Kessel* lived under the assumption that the south *Kessel* had gone down fighting and continued to hold out.

Only after divisional commanders Lenski and Lattmann put Strecker under heavy pressure did the north *Kessel* capitulate two days after the south *Kessel*, on 2 February 1943 at 8.40 am. At the OKH, the last radio message came in: 'The XI Army Corps, with its six divisions, has fulfilled its duty to the last man in heavy fighting. Long live the *Führer*! Long live Germany! Strecker'.

Capitulation

Long grey *columns of* exhausted prisoners gathered and moved to the hinterland. *Obergefreiter* Ernst Panse poignantly painted these last days in his memoirs. From the 9th company of *Pz.Rgt. 24* (24th Pz.Div.), four men were left. They had been stuck completely isolated on the top floor of a house for a long time. To their luck, they had not been hungry, as a food drop had fallen near their 'position'. However, some were wounded; Panse himself suffered from frozen feet. The march through the cold in captivity, was a torture. Upon surrender, they themselves did not actually give a damn about their lives. However, many Russian soldiers proved considerably more comradely than the Nazi propaganda suggested. A certain 'closeness' had developed over time between direct opponents in the city. Often units further behind the front were more brutal than the front troops. Panse was lucky and survived the war.

On the home front, propaganda was running at full speed. The party newspaper the *Völkische Beobachter* mused on 4 February 1943: '*Sie starben damit Deutschland lebe*' and the 6th Army went down 'true to the banner'. *Reichsmarschall* Göring, spoke of 'the unbroken courage' of the 6th Army, and of Stalingrad, as the greatest heroic battle in German history. The ideological position was also underlined: 'Europe is beginning to understand what this battle means'. According to Göring, the German forces had tied 60 to 70 divisions at Stalingrad, preventing a general breakthrough. Although no Waf*fen SS* was serving in Stalingrad, the SS magazine *Das Schwarze Korps* also pulled out all the stops, including a poem by Werner Jansen and an impressive charcoal drawing by *SS-Kriegsberichter* (war-reporter) Wilhelm Petersen. Propaganda minister Joseph Goebbels also tried to stylise the demise of the 6th Army as an example of honour and patriotism. Furthermore, he placed the battle in the context of a 'fight for survival' and introduced the concept of 'total war' (speech 30.1.1943 and 18.02.1943). With this, the 72-day battle had been fought. At the start, 260,000 soldiers had been confined in the *Kessel*, including 10,000 Romanians and 20,000 Russian Hiwis (auxiliary forces). A total of about 40,000 men had been flown out, mostly wounded, and 110,000 men killed, so 110,000 also became prisoners of war including wounded. Of these, 17,000 already died on the march to the POW camps. In total, only some 5,000 Germans returned home; sometimes only after many years. Recently released Russian reports showed that thousands of German soldiers remained hidden in the city after the official surrender date. They no longer offered organised resistance, but hoped for better weather and a breakout westwards. As far as is known, not a single soldier managed to make the harsh journey, let alone survive.

The Air Bridge to Stalingrad Decision-making

On 19 November 1942, the Russian offensive began, which would become known as Operation *Uranus*. The Soviets gathered all their forces and broke through the enemy lines. It did not come entirely as a surprise. *Generaloberst* Wolfram von Richthofen saw the build-up of Soviet forces at the allies' positions and had sent in limited air reinforcements. The Russians had found that the allies were less driven than the Germans, so the choice of attacking Romanian troops did not come by chance.

One of the first to actually observe the breakthrough was Hans-Ulrich Rudel. Rudel was one of Germany's most famous airmen, flying the *Junkers Ju 87 Stuka* (dive bomber) that was widely used as air support for ground troops. After the war, he describes in his memoirs how that day, flying low to stay under the clouds, he was looking for Russian targets and saw vague figures in brown uniforms appear in the distance. They were not Russians, but fleeing Romanian soldiers- many of whom threw away their weapons to run faster. The force of the attack was so great that they had left the positions in a hurry, leaving all the equipment behind. Only some distance away did he observe the Russians. He attacked them with bombs and emptied his machine gun at them, but a single *Stuka* could not stop a Russian army. It was the beginning of a turning point in the war, the Red Army had broken through at a crucial point.

The breakthrough threatened to surround the German 6th Army at Stalingrad and created a situation in which adequate decisiveness was required to make it look as good as possible way out. Three options remained for the Germans. Continue fighting to hold Stalingrad, capitulate, or retreat via a corridor to the southeast and surrender already conquered territory. When the encirclement was a fact, retreat would mean a breakout, which would still have a good chance of success. Encirclement meant defending on all sides and being cut off from supplies of everything an army needed. First and foremost, the 6th Army's needs included food for 200,000 to 250,000 men in the *Kessel*. Yet equally pressing and important to stay alive were military supplies such as fuel for the vehicles, ammunition and medicine. Without these, a surrounded army would soon be doomed or forced to capitulate. If supplies did not arrive in time, the chances of successfully breaking out would dwindle. The men would weaken, morale would drop and there would be insufficient fuel to provide all transport. Without supplies, holding out would immediately fall off the list of possibilities, and a breakout followed by a retreat would leave thousands of wounded behind. Hitler did not want to know about retreat or capitulation. He kept his military apparatus in an iron grip. The only way to comply with his will was an air bridge.

This air bridge is now a historical concept. The most famous air bridge is probably the one from the West to Berlin during the Cold War. It is a politico-military tool to supply an enclosed group of people. The Berlin Air Bridge was particularly political. Yet the first ever air bridge was born out of a military necessity during the Germans' *campaign* against Russia. A year before the 6th Army found itself surrounded by enemy forces at Stalingrad and unable to move, a similar situation had already occurred at Khom and Demjansk. Normally, supplies to the German army went by rail. That was a problem in itself, as German equipment did not fit on Russian rails. A solution to this was found, but in the event of an encirclement, a train could reach the troops. An air bridge provided a viable alternative to this problem, provided that conditions permitted it. Here one has to think air superiority and permissibility by weather. At *Khom* and *Demjansk* it was successful. With relatively small losses, constant supply by air was achieved. The cargo there was brought in not only by transport aircraft, but also by gliders towed by powered aircraft, which of course did not return. One hundred thousand embedded soldiers were supplied with militarily necessary goods, food and medicine from the air for several months. But men were also flown in to help in combat. The wounded were carried off by transport planes that could land there.

Most descriptions of the tragedy at Stalingrad are very brief about the genesis of the decision to organise an air bridge there too. They suffice with the assurance from the supreme chief of the *Luftwaffe*, Hermann Göring, that the air arm would again provide the supplies. This puts all responsibility for the decision on Göring. A relatively recent study by Hayward from 1997, shows that the reality was more complex and that Göring was certainly to blame, but that he was not solely responsible. Questions of decision-making around Stalingrad, do not include the overarching question of primary responsibility for the aggressive invasion of Russia per se.

When news of the Soviet breakthrough reached Hitler on 19 November 1942, he reacted immediately and summoned the *Luftwaffe* leadership to discuss the possibilities of an air bridge. Göring was indisposed and had sent *Gene- raloberst* Hans Jeschonnek as a replacement. Hitler had a step-by-step solution in mind: the air bridge would take care of the army for a limited time and a new army group under *General- feldmarschall* Erich von Manstein would come to the rescue to relieve the 6th Army. Hitler always demanded immediate answers to his questions and Jeschonnek, with the successful action at Demjansk in mind, was quick to assure him that the *Luftwaffe* could handle an air bridge if both bomb-throwers and transport planes could be used. It is sometimes small things that have big consequences. It cannot be proved, but neither can it be ruled out that if Jeschonnek had shown himself to be less servile on this occasion, a trace of doubt might have arisen in Hitler's mind, which would have put later protests against his decision on better ground. A simple calculation could have changed Jeschonnek's mind. Without taking into account differences in circumstances such as weather and enemy strength, it would have quickly become clear to him that the numbers were now quite different. In Demjansk, 150 *Junkers Ju 52* aircraft were needed to supply a hundred thousand men with 300 tonnes of goods per day. For 250 thousand men, some 750 tonnes a day would be needed, and the number of planes needed was therefore 2.5 times larger. The *Luftwaffe* did not have that many planes and gliders. But it was worse, the conditions at Stalingrad were very different, much more complicated. Unlike Demjansk, at Stalingrad there was fierce opposition from the Russian air force and the weather conditions there were wintry and harsh. It is sobering to consider that Hitler's motives for wanting to hold out at Stalingrad were partly personal. He had boasted in speeches to the entire German people that no one could get the Germans out of Stalingrad and that the city bearing Stalin's name was of vital psychological importance. To avoid losing face, he was now committed to holding out. The vital interest of 250,000 men had been subordinated to his personal interest of losing face. Had Jeschonnek reacted less eagerly, he might have thought differently, but Hitler can also be blamed for the fact that people liked to put their money where their mouth was. Without contradiction from the *Luftwaffe* representative Jeschonnek, he therefore did not hesitate and on 21 November he sent *Generaloberst* Friedrich Paulus, the commander on the spot, the order to stand firm despite the threat of encirclement. The train supply had to be maintained as long as possible, orders would follow later on an air bridge.

Indications of an air bridge were met with mixed feelings in the field. The lower commanders argued unsuccessfully for an immediate breakout, because they felt that an air bridge would take far too long and the Russians would become increasingly starry. Hitler and Jeschonnek assumed a limited time, because they believed that Von Manstein would soon break through the encirclement. That this still did not ensure supplies, because they had been failing for some time, is a factor in itself. This not only involved a lack of food and fuel, but also winter clothing was missing and repairs often had to be made by 'cannibalising' (making one usable from two defective aircraft or tanks).

The supreme command on site consisted of *Generalleutnant* Fiebig of *Fliegerkorps VI*, the local *Luftwaffe commander*, in addition to *Generaloberst* Paulus and *Generalmajor* Arthur Schmidt of the 6th Army. Paulus is generally referred to in the literature as a brilliant tactician, but too law-abiding and lacking in personality to go against Hitler's wishes. He had not led such a large unit before. During the consultations now taking place between these commanders, Paulus and Schmidt took the position that they were counting on the *Luftwaffe* to provide sufficient supplies, while Fiebig argued that it was not possible. A complicating factor was also, that a large part of the *Luftwaffe* transport force was at that time deployed in Africa, which Hitler incomprehensibly prioritised. Fiebig's boss was Von Richthofen. The latter shared Fiebig's point of view and made it clear that he considered the idea pure madness. He shouted it to anyone who wanted to hear it, including Göring and Jeschonnek, but did not manage to get through to Hitler, who only belatedly heard his point of view.

For Paul, Hitler's Word Counts

The army command's position was partly motivated by military logic regarding problems with a breakout. Here, factors such as fuel shortages – needed for successful break out - and the strategically better positions of the Russians on higher ground played a role. These technical arguments, put forward mainly by Schmidt, were refuted in heated discussions by other generals. But for Paul, witness to his own statements, only Hitler's order really counted. He had received the order from politicians to stand firm and would stick to it. It is good if soldiers do not allow their own political views to influence their decisions, but even such a rule has its own limits of reality. There are more examples of military leaders who - forced by circumstances - ignored Hitler's orders, which was by no means always remembered by the latter.

As with everything in the Nazi era, ultimate responsibility lay with Hitler. The widely held view that Hitler was surrounded by yes-men is confirmed by Hayward in his aforementioned study of the air war at Stalingrad. In the critical period when a breakout still seemed possible, Hitler's conviction that an air bridge was feasible became stronger and stronger. He was not contradicted by anyone. The objections of the *Luftwaffe* commanders who opposed it did not penetrate him. There was, however, a weak dissent from Jeschonnek who had by now realised his mistake but did not have sufficient weight to assert himself. Opposing opinions were formulated very cautiously.

An objection was encapsulated in a given assent, for example: won territory should not be given up before the army was relieved, although the situation was horrible and the army would certainly be destroyed without a rescue operation. And Göring had also personally assured the *Führer* that the *Luftwaffe* would be up to the task.

At this point - we are still talking about the beginning of the Soviet offensive when the encirclement was not yet a fact - even more personal interests came into play, which ultimately determined the fate of tens of thousands of people. Göring had been informed of the air bridge plans by Hitler, probably immediately after his meeting with Jeschonnek. He agreed without going into the details and only in very general terms. Göring used words like: the *Luftwaffe* will do everything in its power to support this plan. The next day he arrived for a meeting with Hitler and had spoken to his subordinate Jeschonnek. Jeschonnek had made calculations, which showed that transporting large tonnages was doable, but had since found out that he had made a mistake. A small, understandable mistake that, however, had far-reaching consequences. The *containers* in which the goods were to be transported had a designation in tonnage that Jeschonnek interpreted as the quantity in tonnes the container could hold. In reality, the designation indicated the tonnage of the bombs replaced by the containers. No more than about two-thirds of the declared value of goods could be carried by the container. As a result, Jeschonnek's calculations were initially far too optimistic and his claim that the *Luftwaffe* would be up to the task was based on incorrect calculations. The moment he realised the mistake, he did confess it to Göring. But when the latter joined Hitler for the interview, the latter had by now become so entrenched in the air bridge idea that Göring feared for his position if he tried to talk him out of it. And so Göring expressed his personal assurance to the *Führer* that the *Luftwaffe* was up to the task. Also present at that meeting was General Kurt Zeitzler, who had taken the view that the air bridge was not possible, which he had informed Hitler off. But Hitler was not going to give up the idea so easily. There is no written record of the meeting. We know from statements by Zeitzler after the war that he was assured by Göring that it could be done. By then, incidentally, the tonnages promised had already been reduced from 750 tonnes a day to 300 tonnes a day. There was open animosity between the two men and Hitler decided in Göring's favour. From then on, there was no movement in Hitler's position and, as we now know, the only possibility for saving the 6th Army would have been military disobedience on Paulus' part. And Paulus was not the man for that.

There has been much discussion in the literature about tonnages. The 750 tonnes initially talked about was based on the Demjansk experience. Everyone involved was by now convinced that this was an unachievable target. A horrible thought was that the need for supplies would decrease as more soldiers died and more equipment came to a standstill. The figure had to be revised downwards and therefore there was later talk of two other numbers. All in all, it was assumed that 500 tonnes per day was the absolute minimum to keep the Army in a fighting condition. To keep it alive on its own, a minimum of 300 tonnes per day was considered necessary. The Army had the personnel strength of a city like Eindhoven today. 300 tonnes meant 1 to 1.5 kg per man. The 300 tonnes was still guaranteed by the *Luftwaffe*, but ultimately never achieved. One or two days they came close, but the minimum tonnage was never achieved. Some researchers do report one or two landings of over 300 tonnes, but according to the data maintained here by Herhudt von Rohden, this is not correct.

Causes for Air Bridge Failure

There are a large number of reasons for the failure to achieve the stated goals regarding the airlift to Stalingrad. Many of them are intertwined and related. Irresponsible decision-making has already been mentioned, but should not be missing from the list.

Irresponsible decision-making
The decision-making around Stalingrad was carried out dictatorially with too little information and too many personal interests. The dictatorial character is expressed mainly in that opinions contrary to those of the leader were either not expressed or not heard. Of course, in the day-to-day management of a war, you cannot make 'parliamentary' decisions in every situation. However, as a leader, you have to be open to other opinions and weigh them up. It is true, as Zeitzler's statements after the war show, that the decisions were not taken entirely without consultation or without hearing other opinions, but, all things considered, the verdict has to be that there was too little room for dissent and reconsideration during the implementation.

Hitler who, given his earlier politically prestigious statements, could not allow the army to break out while it still could, and Göring, who was initially ill-informed and later too afraid of his position, are two good examples of the personal interests of which tens of thousands fell victim. But the other members of the staff who did not dare to counter properly also fall into this category.

Insufficient capacity
The air bridge would have to be organised with transport aircraft. The backbone of the *Luftwaffe*'s transport system was the *Junkers Ju 52*, the German 'workhorse' in World War II. An incredibly strong and reliable aircraft, ugly and slow, but with an outstanding reputation. The aircraft served the Germans very well throughout the war. But it was unarmed and therefore vulnerable. Many were shot down as a result.

There is quite a lot of juggling with the number of aircrafts in the literature. To give an impression: German internet sources report that the *Luftwaffe* owned 531 transport aircraft in May 1940. US Air Force officer Mike Thyssen, who dealt with the Stalingrad debacle, cites the availability of 550 aircraft for autumn 1942. The total aircraft stock was constantly changing because of losses but also because of new production. Right at the beginning of the war, the large Ju 52 losses in the Netherlands stand out. Although the war in the Netherlands lasted only five days and the defenders were overrun, the Germans suffered hefty losses. Ju 52s were widely used for the air bridges and the Germans lost almost three hundred of them. British online *sources* speak of a year's production lost in this regard. It was large loss that German sources themselves spoke of as a palpable lack of transport capability throughout the war. The air bridge to Stalingrad would undoubtedly have been much more successful without this vicious loss in 1940. The carnage among the vulnerable *Junkers* would not be limited to the invasion of Holland. During the battle for Crete in 1941, the Germans lost about as many. It was the same type of attack with airborne troops and Hitler abandoned this method of warfare from then on.

Since there were too few Ju 52s for the airlift to Stalingrad, bombers were also used. In particular, the *Heinkel 111* was widely used for it. The *Heinkels* had a slightly smaller cargo capacity than the *Junkers*; mainly because they were not equipped for cargo, but for bombs. Other types were also used on a smaller scale, about which more later.

The multi-front policy
After the success in the west against the Low Countries and France, and after the lost battle of England, a front remained there with an

undefeated opponent. Since Hitler's geopolitical plans involved the east, he opened the second front there. But this did not stop there.

Ally Italy had an interest in North Africa. Libya was an Italian colony and Fascist leader Benito Mussolini had plans for conquest in that area, without having the military power to do so. Although it was not on the German agenda, Hitler complied with Mussolini's request for support in his plans to attack the British colony of Egypt. This created a third front in Africa.

The western front required manpower and equipment to control the occupied areas, and (fighter) aircraft to defend the front. The strain it placed on transport capacity was not very great. This was different in Africa. Hitler had to divide his air transport fleet between Africa and Stalingrad. Dividing the aircraft between these two fronts led to there not being enough aircraft for both areas. Some also cite this as one of the reasons for the loss of the Axis powers in Africa, but it also had repercussions on the eastern front.

The strength of the opponent

Germany had absolute air superiority in Russia for a long time. In Demjansk, Russian air power hardly played a role. The tried and tested concept deployed in the overrun of the Low Countries, destroying enemy air force on the ground, had also deprived Russia of its fighter planes. In World War I, a criterion had emerged for an airman's success in the air: he became an 'air ace' on a victory over five opponents or more. Many Germans became airmen in World War II according to this criterion. The average number of personal victories then was also much higher than in the First World War. The Germans achieved relatively easy victories on the Eastern Front because the Russian air force was initially not much of a threat.

The Russian supreme command had crucially increased the war potential with a remarkable action. War production was greatly increased. Even before the Germans had embarked on Operation '*Barbarossa*', they had taken note of this, but apparently did not take it to heart. When German politicians visited Russia, they were shown around huge factory halls with 30,000 workers. The threat of war was already there at the time and the Russians meant it as a deterrent. When the Germans nevertheless attacked, the military was not yet equipped with modern equipment, but production was running. As Christer Bergström shows in his book '*Stalingrad, the Air Battle*' using production figures, Russian war production matched that of the Germans, and later in the war it was even greater. In mid-1942, after the first disastrous months, the Russian air force was modernised and elevated to a self-sufficient weapon, with General Nowikov as commander. This carried out a large-scale reform, adopting a number of tactics from the *Luftwaffe*. As a result, when Stalingrad was attacked, the air was controlled by the Red air force. When the air bridge to Stalingrad started, the Germans initially still had the air superiority, according to some sources.

But this quickly changed, not least also because of the weather situation to be discussed below, in which the Russians, due to their experience were better able to deal with. The danger to the German planes lurked not only in flight. Especially in the final days of the encirclement, when the soldiers almost resented the conditions of cold and lack of food more than the opponent, the Russians carried out air attacks on parked aircrafts. Not only air attacks were to be feared. The front came ever closer and landed aircraft also had to deal with artillery shelling from the ground.

Inexperienced crews
In his book '*The history of Air Cargo and Airmail from the 18th Century*', the historian and vice-president of *Air France Cargo*, Camille Allaz, devoted a short chapter to the phenomenon of military air bridge. He points out that the crews tasked with carrying out the air bridge at Stalingrad were increasingly young and inexperienced. It is an observation that should be accompanied by the side note that this obviously applied to the Russians as well. A war has tens of thousands of casualties, and every time, one sees that as a result, very young and inexperienced people are deployed in circumstances where experience is a necessity of life. Perhaps it was mainly a disadvantage for the Germans, as they had to take advantage of the bad weather conditions precisely to avoid attacks by the Russians. Experienced crews would certainly have been better able to cope with these weather conditions.

Weather

When launching Operation '*Barbarossa*', Germany's self-confidence was so high that it was assumed that it would be a matter of a few months before the Red Army would be defeated. A gross miscalculation. In the winter of '41-'42, the *Wehrmacht* was already stranded before Moscow. Russian losses in human lives were astronomical, but Stalin did not care about human lives and millions of Russian soldiers lost their lives fighting the Germans. Although the Germans initially gained ground quickly in the summer offensive in 1942, things gradually got harder and harder, and when they stopped at Stalingrad, winter gradually set in.

This picture gives a good image of the harsh winter circumstances

The Russian winter was hard on two counts. Firstly, the army was inadequately equipped and trained for winter, whereby combat strength was reduced greatly and soldiers were exposed to extreme cold in their summer clothes. Secondly, the air bridge suffered flight and maintenance problems in operations on snow-covered terrain and especially in snow showers and storms. The army was freezing to death and the supplies for which there was a sharply increasing need as a result were, in fact, severely hampered by the weather.

Most immediate was the impact of weather on the execution of the air bridge. Aircrafts cannot fly in every sort of weather. Navigation capabilities were less developed in 1942 than they are today, but the Germans did have electronic navigation beacons. Today, it is possible to land even in zero visibility. People do not dare to do this under hand control and therefore a zero visibility landing is always an automatic landing. Although around that time, automatic landing was demonstrated by the Germans in particular, it was still experimental and there was no serial production of equipment that would make it possible. However, during the air bridge, some experienced pilots did go very far in a hand-flown landing in extremely low visibility, but this could not be expected of everyone.

Visibility was not the only problem. Pilots had been trained to fly the aircraft from departure to destination without visibility, guided by electronic means. Only at take-off and landing were minimum visibility values required. Severely reduced visibility hindered the execution of the air bridge at Stalingrad in the common fog and in snow showers or obstacles near the runway. When they did manage to take off, in-flight problems were mainly ice problems in the clouds and during snow showers that could develop into blizzards. These conditions were causes that reduced the aircraft's performance and, when things became more extreme, made it impossible to keep it in the air. Solutions to some of these problems were developed for modern aircraft, which did not exist in 1942.

Pilots who had made it through these problems without much harm, the problem of landing on a snow-covered runway awaited at the end. On a well-equipped airfield, this would not be much of a problem, even if the runways were not cleared of snow. But at a wartime airfield under enemy fire, it was an entirely different matter. Wreckage, half-snow-covered, lay like hard-to-separate obstacles around the runway and sometimes on it. There were bomb craters that were not visible through snow, which could cause the landing machine to flip over or the landing gear to break off. During landing, and also after, you could be taken under fire. A landed plane could still be destroyed by enemy fire.

However, it was not just about the operational problems. The availability of transport capacity was not only a matter of sufficient aircraft, but also of sufficient deployability. To achieve this, the aircraft had to be winter-ready before they could be sent to an operational squadron, and extra maintenance was required to prevent wear and tear and war damage. The supreme command, including Hitler, had insufficient insight into the actual availability of aircraft. They worked with the numbers that had been released and were present on paper. When towards the end of the 6th Army's agony, *Generalfeldmarschall* Erhard Milch was sent to Russia by Hitler to put things in order and still try to bring sufficient material inside the encirclement, it became painfully clear to him how things really stood. Milch was a heavyweight whose *career* began in civil aviation with the *Lufthansa* until he was asked by the Nazi regime to build an air force in the 1930s. He was a confidant of Hitler. Only after arriving in Russia did he find out that the strength on paper, which he had worked with until then, was far from reality. Mike Thyssen recounts that when Milch took office at the Stalingrad theatre, he was told that of the 106 aircraft that were at *Zverovo* airfield, only three had landed inside the encirclement that day. There were 48 damaged machines and of the remainder only eight had started, so only three were successful. A sad situation.

This Ju 52 is struggling due to the snow as well

The maintenance staff had no heated *hangars* to tinker in. And it had no experience of working in temperatures of 20 to 30 degrees below zero and 70 km/h winds. Tools froze to the hands. Fingers became numb and developed frostbite. Engines could not or hardly be started. Electric heat guns that were supposed to warm up the motor before they could be started did not work adequately because they could not stand up in the icy wind. Aircrafts coming from warmer regions such as North Africa or the Mediterranean had to be converted to serve in the cold weather. To meet demand, conversions were often delayed and they were sent straight to the front. There, they got in the way of waiting for the overburdened mechanics to convert them, which had to be done anyway. In short, no account had been taken of the Russian winter.

American military historian *major* Roy Lower, in his study of *Luftwaffe* tactics, describes some unexpected sides of the war in his work '*Luftwaffe Tactical Operations at Stalingrad*'. He recounts how a Russian war-fighter helped the Germans fight the problems associated with the low temperatures. Lower supposes the Russian took pride in his superior knowledge and experience when he mixed petrol with lubricating oil and poured it into the oil tank of a *Messerschmitt Bf109*. The Germans flinched when a mechanic first turned the propeller a few turns by hand, and then a pilot crawled into the *cockpit* and started the engine. According to Lower, the Germans expected an explosion after the ignition was switched on, although that was understandable. An explosion caused by petrol in the engine oil could occur if the oil/petrol mixture got onto hot parts when the engine was well warmed up, but not when an in-and-out cold engine was started. So this did not happen: the engine started without any problems. The POW explained that the engine oil became viscous due to the cold and was kept liquid by the petrol. When the engine warmed up, the petrol evaporated on its own. The only drawback was that the lubricating oil would have to be changed more often.

Another trick by the Russian was to place a container of petrol under the open engine compartment, which he then held a burning match to. The flames jumped up and heated the engine. It apparently worked better than the Germans' hot-air guns. The mechanics feared that all the insulation of the wiring would be burnt and expected other damage, but that too did not happen. The question is why the Germans did not achieve better results with the knowledge now acquired. Lower explains this by the lack of experience and too little available time to learn it.

The Russians had more patent solutions to the cold problems, which gave them an advantage over the Germans. By rotating an auxiliary machine connected to the propeller hub for a few turns, they moved the moving parts in relation to each other for a moment, which made the motor catch on more easily. This was done more often and earlier, but then it was one man or a few men spinning the propeller.

A somewhat unexpected problem perhaps in a story about snow and cold, were the periods of thaw, which alternated with frost in November. The thaw caused a mud pool at the unprepared *strips* on the steppe, which made aircraft operations from these landing strips very difficult. The Russians solved this by thawing one part of the terrain and delaying the thaw as long as possible at the other part with, for example, straw. This allowed them to operate longer from the frozen part and earlier from the thawed part.

Sabotage
In his book *'Verrat an der Ostfront',* the historian Friedrich Georg mentions numerous things that would have been the result of betrayal or sabotage. The air bridge did not escape his suspicions either. But nothing in that area has been shown with certainty by him. There were transport shipments with goods that were of no use to the army, for instance only spices or only fishmeal. Many cases of poor organisation are mentioned by him, which could have been deliberate, but could just as easily have resulted from incompetence or overwork. One example is that aircraft deployability was only 10 per cent. It was a fact that *drop tanks* for the Messerschmitt *fighters* to protect the transport arrived only shortly before the fall of the 6th Army, limiting the radius of action. The winterisation of many aircrafts was also delayed and they were brought directly to the area of operations. He further mentions the evacuation of *Tatsinskaya*, the airfield from which the Ju 52s departed. The evacuation did not get under way until the Russians were already there, and many precious

machines were still broken before they could get away. Although everything was in readiness to leave and the pilots were in the planes before the first shells fell on the field, the departure was stopped by orders from higher up.

Especially with the last example, it is very unlikely that this was a result of *sabotage*. Furthermore, the evacuation is described in detail. The Soviets had advanced to near the two supply fields *Tatsinskaya* and *Morosowskaya* and threatened to take them. The supreme command responded in their usual way with the order to hold out until there was no other way. The order came from Göring himself. The local commander had twice requested permission to clear the field, both times rejected by Von Richthofen, following orders he himself had received. Von Richthofen's loyalty to authority has not been questioned so far. So in this case, too, there was no sabotage, but it is clear that common sense played a secondary role.

Konstantin Rokosovski

Vasili Tsjoeikov

Soviet defenders of Stalingrad

Romanian infantry

Surrender of Stalingrad

Paulus at the Red Square in Stalingrad

October 1942: Sturmgeschütz III ausf. B

Train station Stalingrad

Street view Stalingrad

Red Square, Stalingrad 1943

Surviving in the cold

Well-know Wolga song

Focke Wulf Fw 200 b-2 January 1943

Airforce unit 9 of the Red airforce, in front of their YAK-1

The loneliness of the Kalmückensteppe can be felt here

History and Implementation of Air Bridge - Initial Phase

The first flights of the air bridge to Stalingrad took off from Tatsinskaya airfield on 26 November 1942. If there is a lesson to be learnt from the failure of the air bridge, it is the well-known saying 'Better to be half-hearted than to be completely lost'. With only 27 planes leaving on that day, a movement was set in motion that could only be stopped with a major loss of face. Lifting the outbreak ban could still have been done at the time, but Hitler had announced the day before that he would put a highly gifted organiser on the case, and with that announcement, the process was a *fait accompli*. The *Führer*'s publicly declared self-assurance was the momentum of the enterprise. He could not go back, although after a few days he could have invoked the failure of supplies. Perhaps General Rommel arrived just a few days too late. Two days after the start of the air bridge, he came to Hitler asking to be allowed to withdraw from Africa to defend Italy. But like with Stalingrad, Hitler refused to give up on Africa and therefore a large part of the transport capacity had to be deployed there. It was like the famous domino row, it went step by step. Had the decisions on transport capacity for Africa and Stalingrad and been taken at the same time, the consequences would be taken together and would seem greater. Now it went step by step and the consequences for each step separately were smaller. Moreover, those consequences were still masked by the theoretical apprehensions and lagging reports about reality. Hitler himself contributed to the deception by promising SS divisions, which were not (yet) there, and

The Messerschmitt Gigant was supposedly used on occasion, like here at Pitomnik

by ignoring his own losses.

In these early days, the *Führerhauptquartier* was still assuming particularly optimistic expectations that 500 tonnes or more a day could be flown into Stalingrad, while we now know that even the stated minimum of 300 tonnes a day could not be achieved. It was -almost- achieved only a few times. To achieve the minimum average, knowing that there would be days when little or no flying would be possible, the aim on a good flying day had to be more than the minimum. Taking into account maintenance, losses and disruptions in the supply of proper supplies to the airfields, 800 Ju 52s were therefore needed for Stalingrad - regardless of Africa - each capable of carrying about 2 tonnes at a time. Since, in the absence of the Ju's, other types with a lower capacity were used, the number had to be even larger. The two huge transport outputs far exceeded the *Luftwaffe*'s capacity. There were also the ongoing supply tasks elsewhere, which were equally essential. Aircraft had to be taken from everywhere. They were withdrawn from training, including instructors, and furthermore civilian aircraft from *Lufthansa* and government services were used. This was at the expense of the tasks that these aircraft had. The lack of well-trained crews due to lack of training capacity made itself felt for years to come. The communication and mail delivery tasks of civilian aircraft were adversely affected. Greater still was the impact of the withdrawal of bombers and fighters from their offensive duties. They were taken away from all fronts to embark on transport missions after many flying hours. The result was that Von Richthofen, who had to convert his *Fliegerkorps* from an offensive organisation into a transport organisation, ended up with a mishmash of 500 aircraft of various types, nowhere near sufficient for the task. The lion's share of the transport came from the Ju 52. It took some time for all those aircraft to arrive in southern Russia, with jet fuel also having to be brought in. Most had to be prepared for their new task first. Bombers were converted for transport, transport aircraft had to be winterised. Due to time constraints, the latter was quite often waived and the planes went straight to the vote. The most frequently used aircraft were the *Junkers Ju 52, Heinkel He 111* bomber, *Junkers Ju 86, Heinkel He 177, Focke Wulf FW 200, Junkers Ju 90* and *Junkers Ju 290*. This is not an exhaustive list; types of which only a few were used are not mentioned. In addition, escort fighters were deployed.

Although decision-making at the supreme command was poor and left much to be desired, organisation at a lower level was thoroughly

Messerschmitt 109 with long-range tank

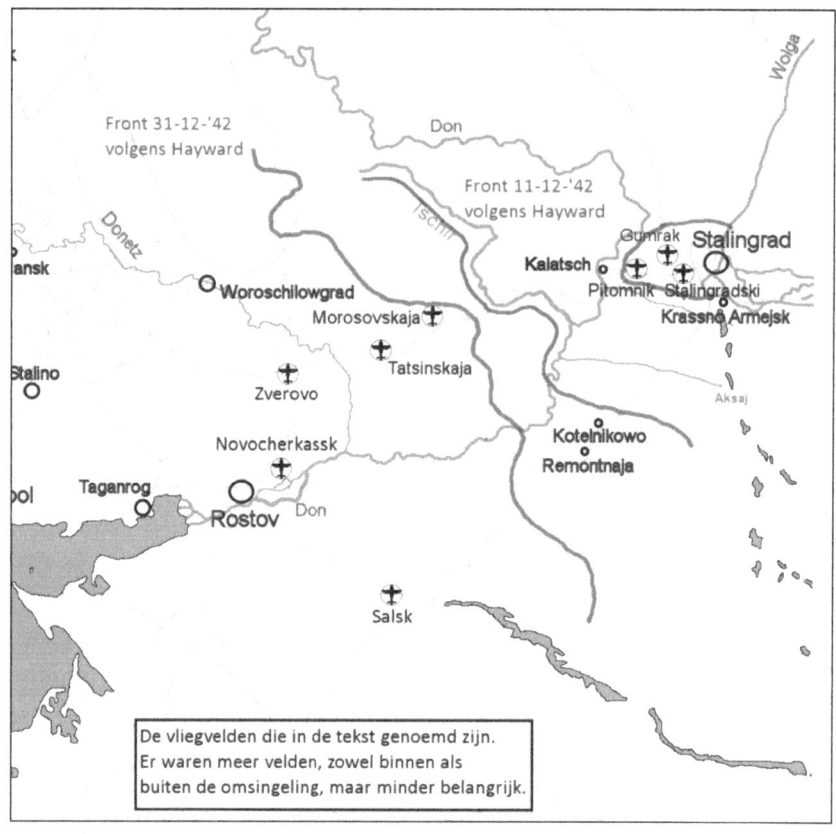

The airports

taken up at its German level. Transport leaders were appointed at the various departure airports, who communicated with each other and coordinated departure times. Electronic equipment was installed at the departure and arrival airports. These were the so-called X- and Y-peilers that worked on reply pulses from the aircraft to interrogation pulses from the ground station. The position was determined on the ground and relayed to the aircraft. A representative of the embedded 6th Army sat at one of the departure ports (*Morosowskaja*) and organised the goods to be transported. An organisation was also set up to pick up the wounded who would be taken with them on the way back, and shelter them, for which a liaison officer was made responsible.

Due to the strength of the Russian air force, flights were conducted in large formations as much as possible, with fighter escorts. Only when the weather was too bad for the enemy fighters to operate effectively, did the formations become smaller or the transport aircraft flew alone. These were blind flying conditions and not every crew was qualified to do so.

One problem with fighter escort was the low action radius of the *Luftwaffe*'s main fighter aircraft. The distance from the main departure ports to the destination was roughly equal to what the fighters could handle, but there were instances of *Messerschmitts being* lost during *escort* due to fuel shortages. One solution would be an external jettisonable tank, which was there for the *Messerschmitt*, but for unclear reasons had not arrived at the relevant squadrons in time. The partial solution adopted was to station some *Messerschmitts* at *Pitomnik*, the main airport within the encirclement. This in turn presented the problem that the aircraft did not always find each other when the *Messerschmitts* flew towards the transport formation. And the Messerschmitts on the enclosed airfields had to be resupplied themselves.

Eleven airfields were used as air bridge departure ports. The most important of these were *Morosowskaya*, *Tatsinskaya* and towards the end, *Zverovo*. *Morosowskaya* had the shortest distance to Stalingrad, 200 km, and was used by the *Heinkel He 111* squadrons. Then came *Tatsinskaya* with 240 km, from which the Ju 52s operated. These fields were also close together. The good fighters were transported to *Pitomnik*, *Gumrak* and later *Stalingradski* airfields. At the time the operation started, there were more airfields available there, a total of seven. The largest airstrip was *Pitomnik*, where initially almost all flights went.

Russians Strike Back

The Russians were not idle and did everything they could to interrupt the 6th Army's lifeline with the hinterland. They set up anti-aircraft guns on the most logical routes to the destination. They sent fighters into the air to attack the transports. They bombed the departure ports as well as the destinations. And they increased the pressure on the surrounded 6th Army. The consequences did not last. Due to all the opposing forces, the requested quantity of goods could never be achieved. The self-imposed minimum target of 300 tonnes per day, which would leave the 6th Army no further than survival and unable to continue fighting, would mean that each day an average of 150 Ju 52s would have to land within the *Kessel*, as the Germans call an enclosed area. Dividing that number neatly over 24 hours, it would mean that every 10 minutes a flying craft had to land, be unloaded, including some of the tank fuel and loaded with wounded if necessary. Taking into account that the other transport aircraft participating in the action had a smaller payload, and the escort fighters also had to land frequently, the time between two landing aircraft had to be even shorter. Only with the availability of several landing fields could the continuing flow of aircraft per field be slightly thinner. It was successful at *Demjansk* at the time; there the 300 tonnes per day was achieved with only one airfield on which to land. But now, at Stalingrad, the 300 tonnes was an absolute minimum and actually the need was twice as great. If someone had calculated it for Hitler, he might have thought differently. So it is not surprising that general Von Richthofen, set for the task to which he himself was deeply opposed, had set as minimum requirements:

1. Continuous transport with sufficient aircraft.
2. A reliable ground organisation (airports, equipment, personnel) outside the ring.
3. Four to six airports within the ring road.

The actions of the Russians mainly focused on these three points. Constant attacks on transports drastically reduced the number of operational aircraft. Anti-aircraft artillery forced the Germans to choose longer routes on days when only low-level flight was possible, allowing more fuel and less cargo to be carried. Moreover, some of the fuel from the aircraft tanks was intended for the army, to keep their motor vehicles running. So with the longer flights, less was left over. The air attacks on the airfields speak for themselves.

Since even the minimum to allow the army to survive was not met, the encircled army weakened rapidly. General Schmidt, the second-in-command inside the *Kessel*, noted at one given moment, that the Russians were walking in front of his lines because the Germans could no longer shoot. All the ammunition they had left had to be

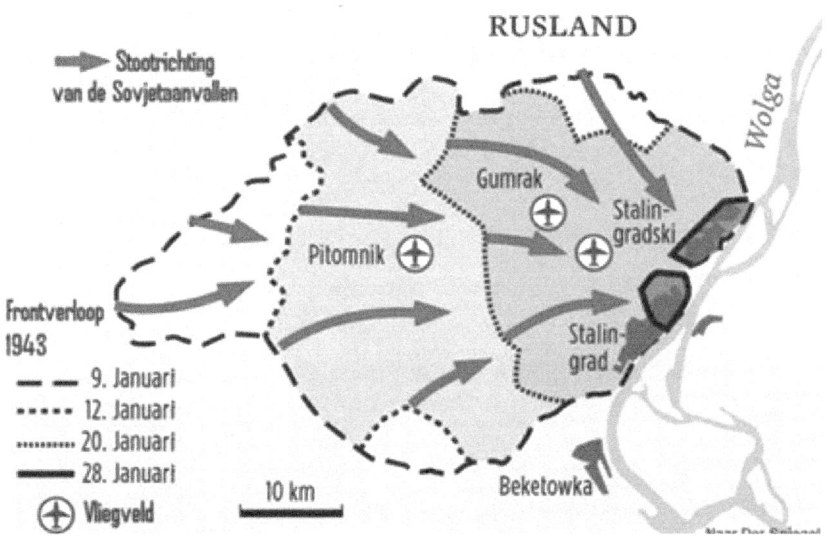

The ever shrinking circle surrounding the 6th Army

kept to defend themselves in case of an attack. Not surprisingly, the Russians were able to systematically shrink the encirclement. The *Kessel* constantly lengthened (see figure). As a result, *Pitomnik* was lost as the first port of attack when it came within Russian-controlled territory, which later happened to *Gumrak*. This was on 21 January, not long before Paulus surrendered. Finally, the smallest of the three fields, *Stalingradski*, was used for a few days. The Russians also targeted the departure ports. *Tatsinskaya* was captured by ground forces. Later, although it was recaptured by the Germans, they eventually had to give it up.

Hard Lesson from Russian Winter

Surely, the first two weeks of the air bridge must have given the Germans something of hope. The graph of tonnages delivered (figure) still shows a slowly increasing picture with peaks and troughs. Yet that pattern did not continue. The main reason for this was the weather. Another factor was that the fleet was not yet at full strength, but even if there had been more aircraft, transport results would not have improved. Winter had set in and it was freezing, but although the low temperature would later become a major obstacle to the whole enterprise, it was not the most important factor at that time. The commanders' war diaries show that especially fog, snow showers and hail showers prevented operations on a large scale. An advantage for the Germans was that the Russians also suffered from the weather. On 8 December, a maximum of almost 180 tonnes was regulated. It was a huge amount, but far too little for an army of 250,000 men in the prime of their lives. The requirement to remain capable of facing the enemy demanded more goods than were being brought in. Fuel, ammunition, weapons, medicine, wound care, not to mention food, were needed in far greater quantities than the average 85 tonnes realised in the first days. It should be noted that initially no food was brought in. It was agreed that the 10,000 horses the army had brought with it would first be slaughtered. Ammunition and fuel were the main goods needed at that time.

German officer Hans-Detlef Herhudt von Rohden, in his book

This crash was not the result of enemy fire

'*Die Luftwaffe ringt um Stalingrad*', paints a vivid picture of what took place at *Pitomnik* base on a day of favourable weather in late November. Herhudt von Rohden was the chief of staff of the *IX. Fliegerkorps* at the time of Stalingrad. He described groups of aircraft which appeared in an almost closed formation at the airfield, where the Russians did not hesitate. They attacked the airfield with bombs and the planes with bullets. It is not mentioned in his text, but it can be assumed that the Germans had taken escort fighters with them. In any case, *Messerschmitts 109* were stationed at the base and an aerial battle of fighters circling each other developed. It hailed downed aircraft, as he noted very evocatively, including many a German transport. Black columns of smoke rose up and in the sky friend and foe could hardly be distinguished. And amidst all that turmoil, *Junkers* and *Heinkels* landed, one after the other, almost peacefully, rolled out and turned away to unload. Then they started again with wounded on board. 660 wounded were brought back that day. These will afterwards consider themselves very lucky to have survived Stalingrad in this way. In normal circumstances, no one chooses to be wounded in war, but in Stalingrad, doctors eventually recognised from experience injuries that the soldiers had inflicted on themselves in order to be eligible for transport home. Not only was that not allowed, but worse, they were summary execution on the grounds of desertion.

Herhudt von Rohden claimed that the Germans still had air superiority at that time. 105 tonnes of goods had been brought in that day and, according to the writer, the people who were taken in were relieved and hopeful that all would be well. They could hold out for a few more weeks with the food. It was a false hope. Eventually, the transport performance had to be increased. The food ran out and then 105 tonnes of supply is not enough.

That the Russian air force had not yet reached its full strength and posed no greater danger to the Germans than the weather conditions at that time is confirmed by Hayward. He describes the same date as a relatively good day because the weather was clear. Many transport planes came in and were attacked by the Russians, who themselves lost 20 planes and shot down only two Ju 52s. In the same period on another day with worse weather, many more aircraft were lost to *crashes due to* the conditions. The Russians hardly played a role in this. Hayward also describes the performance of the ground crews as '*excellent*'. They cleared the runway of snow and wrecks, reloaded the planes and helped them back on their way with wounded on board. Towards the end of the 6th Army's martyrdom corridor, this would

The ground crews had to move mountains in order have the planes be able to land

change. A report written at the time particularly criticised the lack of effectiveness of the ground crews.

A comparison of the strength of the two opponents is necessarily subjective. The opinions of the authors involved can differ, sometimes even the same author reaches contradictory conclusions. For example, Bergström calls the Germans experienced, partly because of the experiences gained during the Spanish Civil War and the Battle of England, while a little later he indicates that the tactics he had called strong of the Germans turned out to be a disadvantage at Stalingrad. He calls the free role the German fighter pilots had in escorting bombers, or - as at the Stalingrad air bridge - transport planes, superior to that of the Russians who stayed close to the planes to be protected when escorting. The German *Messerschmitts* had a habit of patrolling and attacking at high altitude by diving on their target. At Stalingrad, the well-camouflaged Ju 52s often flew very low and were thereby difficult to detect in the be- gin phase, when there was still snow. But the high-flying *Messerschmitts* were conspicuous and betrayed the presence of a transport.

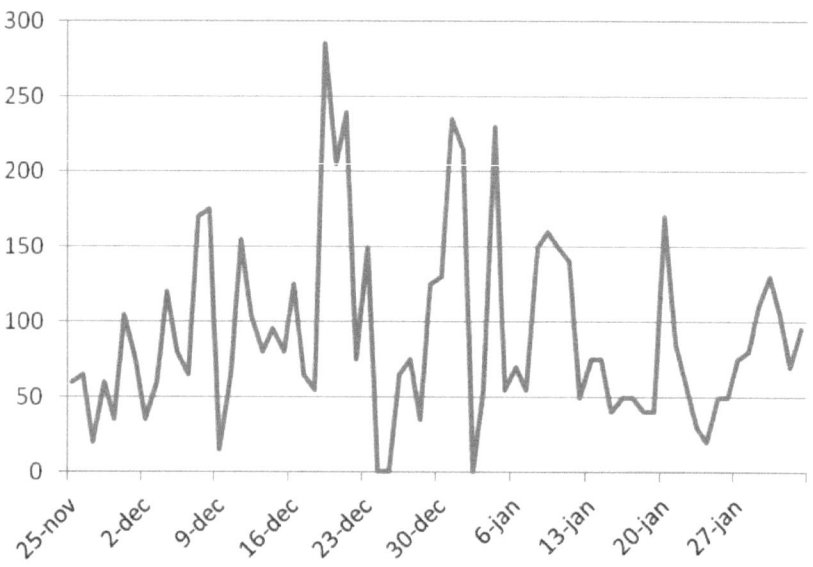

The tonnages flown to Herludt von Rohden

Operation 'Wintergewitter'

Meanwhile, heavy fighting continued on the ground, albeit partly unstructured on the German side. The idea of the air bridge was based on a two-step plan, a short-term air bridge and a dismemberment of the trapped armies. The disengagement attempt had yet to be launched. The Russians were on their way to recapture the Germans' ports of departure and the Germans were defending against them. These actions also required effort from the *Luftwaffe*, which deployed tank attack weapons like the Ju 87 *Stuka*. The *Stuka*, as mentioned earlier, was a dive-bomber and equipped with a terrifying siren that made an indelible impression on people on the ground. Its attack tactics made it particularly effective against tanks. But bombers like the *Heinkel He 111* were needed for these actions as well, the same *Heinkels* that were used for the air bridge. These aircraft could not be used for transport and some were shot down. The Germans, despite their dogged resistance, were driven from the airfields east of the Tschir River. General Fiebig moved his headquarters to *Tatsinskaya* airfield.

As described earlier, on 12 December, an attempt was finally set in motion to relieve the trapped army. Von Manstein had been given the order and worked out the tactical concept. Support from the *Luftwaffe* was limited, given the trans- port task, although some *Heinkels* were temporarily relieved of that task for the sake of the disengagement action.

On 12 December, *Generaloberst* Hermann Hoth opened the aanfall from the town of Kotelnikowo, some 200 km southwest of Stalingrad, initially with some success and followed by a march of over 100 km. The deployment of *Heinkel bombers* was one of the reasons why the quantity delivered at Stalingrad was meagre despite good flying weather, but there again hope of better times was shining and the meagre result was taken at face value. The Russians were taken by surprise, but immediately took countermeasures. When the disengagement force under Hoth had approached fifty kilometres from the encirclement on 19 December, it stalled. According to Von Manstein, the only option then was a breakout of the 6th Army towards the disengagement army, leaving the Stalingrad positions. As soon as contact was made, he would immediately send supplies through the narrow *corridor* thus created.

Yet Hitler decided otherwise. He persisted in holding on to the conquered territories and ordered reinforcements to march, arguing that Paul's army only had fuel for 30 kilometres. It was clear that he was beginning to lose his *grip* on the situation. He ordered the *Luftwaffe* to increase the transport of fuel and food to Stalingrad so that the army could cover the 50 kilometres. It was an unrealistic order, an 'increase' in a situation where even the guaranteed minimum performance was far from being achieved. Despite repeated protests by both Von Manstein and Von Richthofen, Hitler stood firm and only gave permission to break out without revealing the positions at Stalingrad. As always, Paulus obeyed, but saw no possibility of holding out and at the same time countering the disengagement army. Hoth got no further, was even driven back a piece and Paulus stayed where he was. By Christmas, the gunfire could no longer be heard in Stalingrad and it became clear that the disengagement had failed.

A collection of German aircrafts, most likely at Pitomnik

Tatsinskaya in Russian Hands

From the moment Hoth was halted and no initiatives were taken from the encirclement, the fate of the 6th Army was sealed. However, not everyone saw it yet, especially on the German side. From then on, things only got worse for the trapped men. The air bridge functioned, but from the beginning it had not achieved the required level of performance. The enemy, the harsh cold, not enough winter clothing and the poor food situation began to take their toll. Food supplies were slouching as they were replenished only sparsely. The army had taken about 10,000 horses. In this situation, they no longer served any function and were earmarked for slaughter. But for a quarter of a million people, even 10,000 horses are too few to stay alive. A recent article in *die Welt* describes how, in mid-December, troop doctors increasingly had to diagnose the death of soldiers without injuries. Initially, hypothermia, exhaustion or an unknown infection was suspected. To discover the even more dramatic truth, the frozen corpses first had to be thawed in order to perform autopsies. The conclusion baffled the doctors. The diagnosis was: no exhaustion, no infectious disease, it was starvation. The great dying had begun. According to the same article, it became increasingly common for soldiers to drop dead after eating a thin bread soup with a bit of horse meat. The cause was found to be the addition of a little meat fat from canned food, with which the army command wanted to give the men some more calories. It sent them into *shock*.

The Russians pressed on from all sides. Like the Germans, they suffered huge losses but had huge reserves. People lives did not count. Besides exerting direct pressure on the 6th Army, they started advancing towards the two main supply fields *Tatsinskaya* and *Morosowskaya*. The troop movements were detected by the German reconnaissance aircraft, the *Fieseler Storch*. Measures were taken for an immediate evacuation. To prevent equipment and tools from falling into Russian hands, everything was loaded for transport and ground personnel prepared for departure. Once again, a glaring absence of a sense of reality was evident among the leadership in the distant homeland. According to their war diaries, the local commanders cursed the sheltered position at a distance from the generals at the supreme command, who in their offices lacked the feeling for the conditions under which work had to be done in the field. Much to Von Richthofen's frustration, Göring personally intervened in the situation and, in the spirit of Hitler, ordered that they stand their ground. The evacuation was not to begin until literal contact had been made with the enemy. Whatever may be said of the German military in the field, they did more than their duty in order to help the comrades in their plight. The evacuation flights to Stalingrad continued until the last day, despite the circumstances.

What now followed was a drama, described by the historian Franz Kurowski in his book '*Luftbrücke Stalingrad.*' It is the story of the complete failure of the German high command, with Hitler and Göring primarily responsible, and of a starring role for the *Luftwaffe pilots*.

The immediate commander of the air bridge operations, *Generalleutnant* Fiebig, was initially unclear as to which airfield the Russians were targeting, *Tatsinkakaya* or *Moro- sowskaya*. He had set up his headquarters at *Tatsinskaya* and took whatever measures he could to be prepared for the enemy's arrival. All crews were ready at the planes. But he was not yet allowed to move the 180-plus Ju 52s they had there, by order of the supreme command. The '*Befehl ist Befehl*' was taken literally by these soldiers. They remained where they were, until the last minute. Fiebig had permission to move 30 aircrafts not needed for the air bridge with ground personnel to the southern air port of *Salsk*. Only nine left, of which only two arrived. Other than that, he waited for things to come.

Early on the morning of 24 December, at 3.30am, the first Soviet tanks appeared on the outskirts of the town of Tatsinskaya and fired at the military liaison centre. At 3.40am, Fiebig woke up with the message that it was time to take action. At 4.15 he arrived at the airfield. The field was in an uproar. It was a deafening din, engines had already started to get warm. Trucks were driving the latest supplies to the aircraft that were parked close together. Other vehicles drove crews to planes parked further away. It was winter foggy and heavy clouds hung low overhead. There was still no direct contact with the enemy; therefore, by order of the supreme command, no aircraft were yet allowed to leave. The disciplined German soldiers, including the officers, did as they were told. They continued to wait, despite the knowledge that only one thing could happen, the untenable arrival of the enemy assault force. At 5.30 am, the first Soviet shells fell on the field; a Ju 52 took a direct hit and went up in flames. This was the moment Fiebig had been waiting for and he gave the order to launch. A second Ju was hit. The foggy visibility was compounded by light snow swirling from the clouds, hanging just 50 metres above the ground. A serene atmosphere, if it were not for the fact that hundreds of roaring engines could be heard in the background. The propellers started spinning harder, the tumult got worse. The planes set in motion, rushing, fleeing the danger. Within minutes, the field was full of speeding grey shadows in the snow. A total chaos, right behind each other at 20 to 30 metres apart and rows thick, the machines took off in the whipped snow, leaving no hand in sight. The pilots had to trust that the machine would keep going for them. They started slightly apart to avoid a collision as much as possible. That would mean their irrevocable end. Cannon roars, flashes of light, clouds of smoke, it was hell. There were casualties, planes were shot out of the sky. Since they had already left the ground, they made no other casualties in the process. One by one, the survivors disappeared into the clouds. In the space of twenty minutes, it was over. They were still under fire, but pretty much all the planes had disappeared or been shot down.

General Fiebig had kept back a Ju 52 for himself and his staff. After the fleet left, the buildings and bunkers were on fire. He received the almost superfluous report that the enemy had appeared in the town and that there was no stopping them. He himself passed on another report to Von Richthofen that he had decided to leave. A last Ju hurried across the runway and took to the air. The last *Storch* also departed. At a quarter past six, Fiebig's plane also took off. Visibility had improved slightly and increased to 500 metres, but the cloud ceiling had dropped to 30 metres. 106 Ju 52s and 16 Ju 86s had been saved. But the loss of 56 aircrafts was nevertheless an extremely sensitive blow to the efficient running of the supply of Stalingrad. The loss of aircrafts also meant a loss of the people carried, pilots, ground crew and wounded. Indispensable equipment was on board and now destroyed. General Fiebig had to defend his order to defect to the command and explain to them that he could assume that the shelling indicated the immediate proximity of the enemy, although he could not see them directly in the dark due to the prevailing weather conditions. A strange situation when it is remembered that the loss of men and materiel was a direct consequence of the incomprehensible order to hold out, taken 2,000 kilometres from the scene of action. Those responsible for this nonsensical order did not have to defend.

It was yet another blow to a bizarre venture for which no hope was left. But they did not give up. The base of operations was now shifted to *Salsk*. Against better judgment, the bridge was maintained. There was no progress; things got worse in every conceivable way. From the new departure location, a greater distance had to be covered to reach Stalingrad. As this required more fuel, less cargo could be carried. The enemy now had longer time to attack and the distance was too great for fighter escort along the whole route. As Hayward points out, it even created an un-expected new problem for the Germans, combined with bad weather. Since longer distances had to be flown, the Germans chose fixed routes, varied less. This gave the Russians an opportunity to set up anti-aircraft defences in places where the Germans always passed. Dense fog which, while increasing navigation problems for the Germans, provided better protection against the enemy under normal circumstances, did not help now. The Russians knew where they were coming and because they were flying low, when they heard the distinctive sound of the engines, they could fire blind with a good chance of success.

Luftwaffe losses increased rapidly, partly directly due to enemy action, partly due to weather. Ice-covered wings always pose major flying problems. Wings covered in ice can only provide the necessary lift if the speed remains above an ever-increasing minimum value. But even if the lift was sufficient, stability and control problems could still occur. The men of the *Luftwaf- fe* made great sacrifices to help their comrades in the increasingly close encirclement. There, fatalities reached immense proportions, caused by the enemy, but more so by the weather and food shortages. Pointless losses; pointless for the threatened, the rescuers and pointless for the adversary.

Fighter Jets on *Pitomnik*

As we saw earlier, a group of Me-109 fighters was stationed at *Pitomnik* for practical reasons. On the one hand, it partially solved the problem of the low flying range of the fighters when *escorting* the transport planes; on the other, it was a direct protection against Red air force attacks. The difficult weather conditions, combined with the constant threat and attacks from the Russians, not only had a

A crashed Messerschmitt 109 that clearly left an impression. Multiple photos were taken, all from different angles. In the left corner photo, it seems like parts have been taken

disastrous effect on the transport aircraft, but also reduced the effectiveness of the fighters. The fighter group's strength was officially 12, but actual deployments rarely exceeded three. Crashed and damaged aircraft were used as a source of spare parts. Some *Stukas* were stationed there as well.

Feldwebel Kurt Ebener was the fighter pilot who made a name for himself there. He became an air ace who caused the Soviets 33 casualties in 18 flying days. It should be noted that the purpose of the fighter group was not to eliminate as many enemies as possible, but to protect the airbase and transports. His story - reproduced here as an eyewitness account - not only shows the work in the air, but, since he was stationed within the encirclement, the hideous reality of the 6th Army's fate as well. Operating at the enclosed airbase was considered so psychologically taxing that the occupation of the escadre consisted purely of volunteers. Pilots served there for only a few consecutive days and were then relieved. Only Ebener was there continuously for a full month.

Having signed up for it, he took off on 16 December from *Morosowskaya* in a formation of two *Messerschmitts* towards Stalingrad. On the way, they gave fighter support to Hoth's disengagement force and then flew on to the landing site within the encirclement. In the middle of the snow-covered landscape, the airstrip running east-west could be recognised by the parked aircraft, whose *camouflage* colours in the snow could no longer be used. The anti-aircraft guns at the edge of the field also stood out. As soon as they landed, both machines were instantly refuelled. The pilot he had come with immediately started back in an escort formation, with another pilot about to be relieved, for a returning group of Ju 52s. While Ebener's was getting acquainted with his new duty station, he saw the death of a comrade who, in the plane with which he himself had just arrived, was burnt down in a dogfight with Russian fighters. In the days that followed, he experienced the tactics of the Russians who stayed at a great distance from the airfield as long as the *Messerschmitts* were in the air to protect the field, but pounced on the defenceless fighters as soon as they turned on for landing and attacked again during take-off. He became well acquainted with the *Messerschmitt*'s characteristics, which mostly lost in the circle fight, but were faster than the Russian opponents. He also gained experience with his aircraft's warning systems and knew how far he could still go when the red fuel light came on to indicate it was almost through, often in the middle of a battle. Many times he landed with barely a drop left in the tank.

It had become a war without glory at Stalingrad. Here, no triumphant stunt work after a victory, no victory signs on the keel plane to indicate the number of opponents downed. Not even elated greetings when returning from a successful hunt. What mattered was survival, looking forward, waiting for the next attack.

The days before Christmas were no flying weather and Ebener wanted to visit his brother, who was stationed nearby. As the car kept getting stuck in the snow, he sent the driver back and continued on foot. When he arrived, he did not meet his brother and had to spend Christmas with unknown men; a Christmas that, despite the lack of family, he experienced as one of the most meaningful of his life. The retreat into the dark night was an experience he would not forget. It was only six kilometres and it was not difficult to find the right direction. The swelling of aircraft engines at the airport could be clearly heard. The occasional ignition of the approach lights made the objects he encountered on his way stand out clearly against the fire-red horizon. They were windblown accumulations of snow on the barren steppe against everything that had resulted from the war. Burnt-out tanks and other vehicles, as well as corpses of horses and, above all, human corpses. The closer he got to the airfield, the more corpses he came across. He had known it, he had seen them often enough from the air, stumbling, crawling to reach the hoped-for rescue with their last efforts; efforts that too often proved insufficient. What better way to demonstrate the demoralised state of the army than to completely ignore all those dead bodies around the airbase?

Yet the battle was not yet given up. During an air battle, he came up against a superior force of fighters he did not know. They turned out to be American fighters of the *Bell P 39 Airacobra* type, supplied to the Russians by the Americans. He survived the encounter only by throwing his *Messerschmitt* to the ground on the airfield after several wild manoeuvres, by way of landing. As he fled from it, the Russians chased right over him. That day, he did not get back to flying and sought out his brother again. There he was introduced to the other weapon the Russians had deployed to undermine German morale: the loudspeaker messages calling for surrender and fine promises of treatment in POW. None of the emaciated German fighters, unaffected by injuries from frostbite and shelling and with no hope of a good outcome, surrendered. His brother was killed a few days later.

Kurt Ebener survived the hell of Stalingrad. But on 23 August 1944, it was over for him too. The successful fighter pilot, promoted to *Oberleutnant*, was shot down in flames near Paris by a force of six *Republic P 47* American *Thunderbolts* and about 20 *Spitfires*.

Ju 52

The loss of *Tatsinskaya* weighed heavily. The area southwest of Stalingrad, which included the two fields of *Tatsinskaya* and *Morosowskaya*, was now the battleground with varying degrees of success for both sides. Soviet pressure on *Morosowskaya* was high and the commander on the spot, *Oberst* Kühl, decided to immediately move the *Heinkel* and *Stuka* fleet to Novocherkassk, not far from Rostov, when he heard of the *Tatsinskaya* debacle. He wanted to avoid a repeat on his field and therefore ignored the order to leave only at the last minute. *Morosowskaya* remained in German hands for the time being, and

Kühl himself had stayed behind to direct operations there. He had his planes carry out attack flights on the Soviets and most of the fleet returned after two days. On 28 December, German forces managed to recapture *Tatsinskaya*, and Von Richthofen immediately ordered it to be reestablished as an airlift base. However, it was to no avail. Both fields remained under heavy Soviet pressure, the Ju 52 fleet remained at *Salsk* for the time being, and at *Morosowskaya* the alert status remained. Everything there was in readiness for immediate departure. This was how they entered the new year.

An die im Raum von Stalingrad eingekesselten Offiziere und Soldaten der deutschen Wehrmacht

Soldaten und Offiziere der im Raum von Stalingrad eingekesselten deutschen Armee!

Einen ganzen Monat seid Ihr jetzt schon umzingelt; ein dichter Ring von Sowjettruppen hält Euch umfaßt.

Ihr habt auf die Hilfe der Truppen gehofft, die Hitler in aller Eile im Raum nördlich von Kotelnikowo zusammengezogen hat.

So wißt denn, daß wir diese deutschen Truppen vernichtend geschlagen haben.

Im Raum von Wassilewka—Werchnje-Kumski—Klykow hat die Rote Armee sechs deutsche Divisionen, darunter drei Panzerdivisionen, überrannt und zerschlagen, die Überreste dieser Truppen um 60—85 Kilometer zurückgeworfen und in diesen Kämpfen 278 deutsche Flugzeuge, 427 Panzer und 221 Geschütze vernichtet. Allein an Toten haben die Deutschen hier 17 000 Mann verloren. Eure Hoffnungen, aus der Richtung Kotelnikowo Hilfe zu bekommen, sind damit zuschanden geworden.

Ihr habt gehofft, daß Euch die Truppen heraushauen werden, die Hitler in aller Eile im Raum von Tormossin zusammengezogen hat.

So wißt denn, daß auch diese Truppen vernichtend geschlagen und aufgerieben sind.

Die Rote Armee ist auch am mittleren Don zur Offensive übergegangen und hat in den Kämpfen zwischen dem 16. und 27. Dezember 58 000 deutsche Soldaten und Offiziere vernichtet, 56 000 Mann gefangengenommen, 305 Panzer, 2128 Geschütze, 310 Munitions- und Lebensmittellager erbeutet bzw. zerstört.

Unsere Truppen haben die Städte Millerowo, Tormossin, Tazinskaja und Morosowski erobert.

Während eines Kampfmonats im Raum von Stalingrad und während der zehntägigen Kämpfe am mittleren Don haben die deutschen Truppen

insgesamt 169 000 Mann an Toten und 128 000 Mann an Gefangenen sowie 2663 Panzer und 5356 Geschütze verloren.

Eure Hoffnungen, aus der Richtung von Tormossin Hilfe zu bekommen, sind ebenfalls zunichte geworden.

Ihr habt schließlich gehofft, durch die Transportflieger Hilfe zu bekommen.

Soviet propaganda to break the German morale

The Calamity Continues

1943 began catastrophically for the Germans. On 1 January, Fiebig ordered *Morosowskaya* to evacuate because Soviet troops were getting too close. This time he ignored the order to hold out. The *Heinkel* bomber *fleet* again left for *Novocherkassk*, to stay there and carry out supply missions from there. In doing so, they encountered the same problems as their colleagues from the Ju 52 division at *Salsk*, as here too the distance to Stalingrad increased by some 130 km.

The situation inside the encirclement had become dramatic. This was obvious to every person involved, including the enemy. Every departing plane was overloaded with sick and wounded, and any who were given a seat by virtue of their serious injuries were better off than their healthier comrades who had to stay behind. Wounded people dragged themselves to the airport with their last efforts in the hope of being saved by a flight home. Many did not make it and the road leading to it was littered with frostbitten corpses for which no further effort was even made to remove them, let alone bury them. No grave could be dug in the frozen ground. Aircraft crews had no choice but to keep the desperate out of the aircraft with gun in hand. Internet sources report that sometimes planes crashed immediately after take-off due to overloading. It had nothing to do with the will and determination of the *Luftwaffe*, as they fought on, made sacrifices and deployed new initiatives. When *Salsk* too began to be endangered by the advancing Soviet forces, another favourable place had to be found

Corpses of fallen soldiers, frozen in the position they died in

to continue air bridge operations for the Ju 52. Suitable air ports that were an acceptable distance from Stalingrad in German-controlled territory were no longer available. The only possibility was to build a new field and Fiebig personally flew around in a *Storch* reconnaissance plane to pick out a flat terrain. He found one near the town of Zverovo. Within days, a whole new airfield was created, complete with runway, buildings, maintenance hangars, connections and supply equipment. Although the distance to Stalingrad was only just within range of the Ju 52, they were safer here than on any of the other fields.

On 7 January, the Russians sent a negotiating delegation to Paulus with an *ultimatum* to surrender. It described the hopeless situation of the besieged troops and gave conditions for a surrender. It promised that every soldier would be allowed to keep his uniform and decorations, treated well in captivity and given sufficient food. After the war, all would be able to return to Germany.

Paulus wanted to accept, but first contacted Hitler. Most historians hold that Hitler had few illusions about the fate of the 6th Army at that moment, although he had promised a second disengagement attempt in February. Still, he refused to allow capitulation, aiming to force the Soviets to hold troops at Stalingrad, which would relieve the other fronts. If he had any doubts at all he did not share them with Paul; he only gave the order to hold firm and Paulus again obeyed. The 6th Army was sacrificed, as the Russians had already won the battle.

Thereupon, the Russians intensified their attacks and put into practice an already formed plan, which involved dividing the encircled area into two parts. Despite their poor condition, the Germans defended themselves fiercely and were able to hold up the action for a long time. However, there was no stopping them and by 15 January the *Kessel* had been divided into two smaller areas. 16 January, Russian troops stormed *Pitomnik* airport, the main supply port for the surrounded army.

Paulus had seen it coming and did what he could. He sent the chief of the ground teams, *Generalmajor* Wolfgang Pickert, to Von Richthofen to convince him of the seriousness of the situation. The commitment of all concerned is evident from his account. Soviet attacks on the field were already in full swing when Pickert left at dusk in a *Heinkel He 111*. Long-range artillery had been deployed and the Red Air Force was constantly carrying out bombing raids. Around him, grenades were exploding and the flashes of fire from enemy guns were clearly visible. Losing the landing site would be disastrous for the army, he testified. An army of this size could not be supplied by *drops*, which would be the consequence. There were other fields, but *Pitomnik* was by far the most suitable due to the facilities available and the size of the runway. He insisted on returning and eventually got permission to do so. He even wrote farewell letters to his family. When his *Heinkel* arrived at *Pitomnik* and did not receive the proper landing signs, the pilot returned to *Novocherkassk*. Pickert later learned that by the time he was due to arrive, the field was already virtually in Russian hands and the *Heinkel* would probably have been shot to pieces had the landing gone ahead. The reconnaissance aircraft and *Messerschmitt fighters* present at the field had already diverted to *Gumrak*, which had now become the main supply port. The field turned out to be far inferior to *Pitomnik*; the runway was short and poorly maintained, and many planes had overturned during the landing.

Erhard Milch's Attempt

According to many, Hitler no longer had a realistic idea of the real situation in Russia. This was reported, among others, by front-officer Winrich Behr, who had been sent by Paulus to Von Manstein to give him first-hand accounts of the seriousness of the situation. Von Manstein forwarded him to Hitler with instructions to tell the same story as to him. He was received by Hitler and had an interview with him. During this conversation, Behr got the impression that he was not really getting through to the *Führer* and that he was living in a fantasy world of maps and strategic plans that no longer had much to do with the real situation. But he did respond.

Hitler decided to send *Generalfeldmarschall* Erhard Milch to Russia to increase the supply performance and make the enlisted army last as long as possible. Milch had spearheaded the formation of the *Luftwaffe* before the war, reporting directly to Göring. He was an able organiser and political heavyweight, and was given far-reaching powers by Hitler. Paulus had let Hitler know that without an increase in supplies, the situation was not sustainable until mid-February, the time when the latter had planned a second disengagement attempt. He even demanded well-equipped troops be brought in. He too apparently no longer had a realistic view of the real possibilities. For Milch, receiving the order coincided with the news of *Pitomnik*'s fall.

For the Germans, the problems piled up. *Gumrak* was a much smaller field than *Pitomnik*, with an unprepared runway and initially no electronic navigation aids. Anticipating *Pitomnik*'s fall, Von Richthofen had wanted to start preparing *Gumrak* earlier to accommodate transport planes with sufficient ground organisation. Even so, Paulus had set up his headquarters there and did not want to draw the attention of the Russians to the field by developing construction activities there. As a result, after *Pitomnik* fell into the hands of the Russians, the field was unusable for a few days and supplies had to be delivered by air drops. This was sometimes done in special containers on parachutes, but other times simply in wooden crates that were pushed overboard. Many of these were not found or recovered. There was no fuel to run vehicles and the men were too weakened to pick them up on foot.

Von Richthofen and Fiebig understandably perceived Milch's arrival as a misjudgement of their own performance. They feared becoming the scapegoat for the developing debacle that they themselves had predicted the moment the idea of an air bridge was brought up. There was, Fiebig wrote in his war diary, not much more to organise about the *drops* that were now underway. Milch regained their appreciation when he went straight back to work after suffering serious injuries in a car accident. His car was hit by a train when he was on his way to Zverovo to attend to the situation in person. Two soldiers were killed in the accident and it was a miracle that Milch survived. It was a shock for Milch when he received a report on the deployability of the fleet immediately after taking office. The numbers he faced were dramatically different from those the supreme command reckoned with. The size of the fleet was known very precisely, but not its condition. The different authors quote different numbers on this point, but the similarity in them is that all quote a much lower number of deployable aircraft than what was known to the supreme command. According to Hayward, operational availability was down to 20 per cent. Of the 27 *Focke Wulf FW 200 Condors*, aircrafts designed for civilian scheduled services, only one was deployable. Much had been expected of the type, as it was large transport capacity, but it was not built for war conditions and proved too vulnerable. And the reliable Ju 52s and the *Heinkels He 111* also needed a lot of maintenance, more than was apparently anticipated. As the foremost reason for this, weather was again cited.

Despite Milch's decisiveness and far-reaching powers, it was too late. Von Richthofen complained that he could have achieved much better results earlier if, like Milch, he had been able to bypass bureaucracy. One calamity followed another. The situation around *Gumrak* was disastrous. Sov- jet troops were several kilometres away, putting the field directly within artillery range. A landing was therefore life-threatening and this was exacerbated by the poor condition of the runway full of craters, wrecks and covered in snow. Many inexperienced crews did not dare to take the landing and turned around. When a landing did take place, ground organisation was found to be lacking and the crew had to unload the goods themselves. The desperation of the wounded soldiers who hoped to be flown home grew as did the psychological strain on the crews who had to keep them off the plane with a heavy hand. Milch took a host of measures and considered new ideas that nevertheless could not ultimately increase transport performance. He made sure that everyone knew about and used the cold-start procedure for the engines, did his best to give personnel better protection from the cold by having barracks, which had been ordered earlier, brought fighters to Stalingrad with long-range tanks and considered using gliders to multiply transport capacity. This idea had been previously considered by Von Richthofen and Fiebig, and rejected for a number of good reasons. Not the least of these was that the large cumbersome and slow towing combinations were an even easier prey for the Russian air force than the slow *Junkers*. Moreover, conditions at Stalingrad were such that they would not be able to take off there to be brought back. The latter was not a problem for Milch who, however, eventually abandoned the idea and released the gliders to be deployed elsewhere. So not everything Milch came up with ran smoothly. For instance, the baracks urgently needed to protect personnel from frostbite arrived at *Zverovo* weeks late, as more pressing matters took priority in transport. Those 'urgent matters' were the gliders, after he had already abandoned the idea.

A picture of a leadership in confusion emerged. Success has many fathers, failure is an orphan. At the level of generals, things began to be blamed on each other and a controversy arose between the army and the air force. It was forgotten that most *Luftwaffe*

The mighty Focke Wulf FW 200, here looted by the Soviets at Pitomnik

commanders had warned of the consequences from the moment the idea of air bridge was mooted. Typical of this situation was the report of Major Erich Thiel, the commander of a *Heinkel squadron*, who was sent by Milch to *Gumrak* on 19 January to report on the operational skills and provide an assessment of suitability for day and night operations.

Thiel prepared a comprehensive report of his findings on 21 January. He painted the condition of the snow-covered runway and the dangers of enemy attacks. He described the many bomb craters on the runway and counted thirteen aircraft wrecks including a Me-109 which was at the end of the runway and posed a great danger to inexperienced crews. He reported how his own plane was shelled by enemy artillery immediately after landing. For these reasons, he believed it was impossible for the Ju 52 to approach *Gumrak* except in bad weather, as enemy activity would then be less or non-existent. He cleared the field for day landings, but for night landings only by experienced crews. The after-dark lights had not always worked because of the danger posed by enemy attacks. He warned that if any wreckage remained on the runway, flying operations would be halted for the whole of the rest of the night as the ground organisation would not be able to clear it due to enemy shelling.

Immediately after the landing, Thiel had a meeting with Paulus, at which his Chief of Staff, *General* Schmidt, and others were also present. Here he expressed his opinion about the suitability of the field and the lack of the necessary ground organisation, and assured them of the willingness of the flying personnel and the *Luftwaffe* leadership to do their utmost. To this, Paulus replied in very sombre terms. It was already the fourth day in a row that people had been given nothing to eat. He described how soldiers plunged into the carcass of a horse, cracking open its head and devoured its brains. Every machine that lands, he said, saves the lives of a thousand people. And he complained that the *Luftwaffe* had promised that care could be carried through by air. He added that if he had been told that supply by air would be impossible, he would have broken out while he could. Now it was too late. Schmidt interfered in the conversation here with an excited tone, reproaching the *Luftwaffe*, and even using terms like treason. It had apparently been forgotten that it was they themselves who wanted to go ahead with the air bridge against the advice of the *Luftwaffe* chiefs. Paulus now did not want to leave the decision to land to the crews of the planes themselves, whether they were under fire or not. Landing was mandatory, even if the aircraft would be lost in the process. A refusing crew had to be dragged before a court martial.

It was agreed that the field would remain operational throughout the night. The places where the goods could be dropped were identified and they would be fitted with lights so that they could be recognised at night.

When Thiel had returned to his plane, it was found to be badly damaged by Russian shelling. The flight engineer had been killed. Unloading, 11 hours after landing, had not yet begun and even the fuel so urgently needed was still in the tanks. Again, artillery fire was the reason for this. Several crews had earlier reported to him that they had had to take the unloading in hand themselves and that the goods piled up were left unguarded for a long time and looted by passing soldiers.

Russian aircrafts were active and besieged the airfield in formations of three and four fighters. It was a clear night and any land-

A Heinkel in the snow

ing aircraft would be brought down mercilessly. The Russians took care to stay out of range of the anti-aircraft guns and cruised at an altitude of 500 m. On the approach of a German transport, the approach lights were lit. It was an unmissable aiming point. Immediately it hailed bombs on the field. Landings were impossible, the aircraft would be destroyed by the bombs. Therefore, only a brief ignition of the lights showed the aircraft the position of the airfield to ensure at least the ejection of the load. By 11 o'clock the Russians disappeared, probably because the now persistent light snowfall was too much for them. Then the way was clear to land and a Ju 52 came in. The plane unloaded and was able to take off again within half an hour. It took 26 wounded back to *Zverovo* and Thiel himself had stepped in. He too had noted an impending panic among those who could not come along.

Efforts to improve *Gumrak*'s landing capacity were successful. Pilots were instructed to continue landing during light artillery shelling, only if it was too heavy were they allowed to shed containers. Ground organisation improved, the runway was cleared of obstacles, lighting and electronic navigation improved, as did transport performance. On what followed next, historians disagree. Hayward reports that on 23 January, Fiebig received a radio message from the army urging him not to send any more planes because contact with airfield had been broken. It was said to concern the fall of *Gumrak*. Kurowski places the abandonment of *Gumrak* earlier, on the 21st, and the relevant radio message received on the 23rd was said to concern the *Stalingradski* field, which had meanwhile been commissioned. Indeed, Hayward also puts the fall of *Stalingradski* on the 23rd, a few hours after *Gumrak*. Be that as it may, Russian forces had first invaded *Gumrak*. It began with the intensification of artillery fire that destroyed the electronic equipment that the planes used to could enter, was wiped out.

The fall of *Gumrak* was foreseen by Paulus. His troops, crippled by cold, weakened by lack of food and in static positions by lack of fuel, were no longer able to cope with the increasing Soviet pressure. These troops pressed on more and more, gaining ground in the process. Paul's cry for help to Hitler, in which he still expressed full confidence in the leadership, was answered by the latter with the order not to surrender and to fight with all who were still capable of doing so. By doing so, they tied up the Russian troops and thus contributed gloriously to the inescapable German victory.

In any case, *Stalingradski* was the last usable landing strip within the encirclement. Seeing the demise of *Gumrak* ahead of time, they had already started preparing the field for air bridge. On 22 January, it was declared operational. However, when the *Heinkels* tried to land there, six crashed due to the bomb craters and thick snow. Milch was convinced that *Stalingradski* could only lead to a greater loss of aircraft and banned night landings. Only the Ju 52s were allowed to land in daylight, although they were also allowed to refrain from doing so at their discretion. Supplies had to be dropped for the most part. The Germans fought for all they were worth, but only achieved increasing tragedy. After the fall of *Gumrak*, *Stalingradski* was stormed by Soviet troops as well and they no longer had a landing field within the very small and bisected encirclement.

The last Ju 52 flight to and from *Stalingradski* is described in detail and it is again a story full of heroism and tragedy. The pilot described what he found after landing; no more ground organisation. He mentioned the optimistic attitude of the Flak soldier who still believed in an upset and apparently no longer had a real picture of the harsh reality. He described the half-dressed people dragging themselves through the snow to the machine in only some of their suits, with frostbite wounds, and how he could not bear to take only seventeen with him, and thus turned away from those he had to leave behind, who were facing certain death. How, on a whim, he had a seriously injured person pulled out of a crashed *Heinkel*, which had been left behind when the crew got away as quickly as possible after an attack to catch a departing plane. The other wounded had managed to leave the wreckage under their own power, but this man was unable to do so.

The number of people who could return with them was based on the tactical assessment about the *Junkers'* climbing ability and manoeuvrability to escape the enemy after take-off. The enitre time they were on the airfield, they were shelled with artillery fire and Russian fighters carried out diving attacks. They shot at the already crashed *Heinkel*. During a combat break, he decided to take his chances and leave, believing that if he waited any longer he might be shot to pieces himself. Despite initially intending to get away at high speed flying low, he eventually decided by feeling to go for a higher altitude. In doing so, he had discovered a bank of wool, which he could use as cover. After he had reached 3000 m altitude, circling to avoid passing the front at low altitude, an enemy fighter appeared. Immediately he plunged down towards the clouds at full throttle, passing the front in the process. With the fighter on its heels, the anti-aircraft guns fired unceremoniously. The Russian had arrived at too high a speed and fired his machine guns, but hit nothing. He flew by and had to turn back to attack again from behind. Meanwhile, the Ju had reached the clouds. To his dismay, the pilot noticed that it was only a very thin layer and that he had shot out again immediately on the underside. A cat-and-mouse game now started with the Russian above the clouds and the German below and vice versa. At last the Russian turned away, probably due to lack of fuel. The flight arrived safely at *Zverovo*.

On the 24th, in the face of the situation where care could only be provided by *drops* and where no more wounded could be carried off, Paulus again asked Hitler for permission to surrender, which was again refused.

Some within the encirclement found the courage and energy to organise the *drops* and prevent the crates and *containers* from falling into Soviet hands or ending up somewhere too dangerous to pick them up. Sites were found in both parts of the surrounded area, marked with a light beacon and equipped with a radio beacon so they could be found. Nevertheless, much was lost. The *Luftwaffe leaders* felt committed to helping their comrades as best they could. The entries in their war diaries show a deep commitment. That of the individual crews is evident from their willingness to continue carrying out the dangerous flights, but it was all to no avail.

Infantry Stalingrad

Protection against the cold

Capitulation Stalingrad, general Paulus surrenders

Silent witness to the battle

Traffic sign Stalingrad

A city in ruins was what remained

Soviet infantry, Stalingrad

German defense position, with MG-42

152 mm shells, Red Army

German mortar next to Soviet T-34 tank

The tennis racket of Stalingrad

The city from the sky

Hanged Soviet partisans

Memorial in present day Wolgograd

Disabled Soviet T-60 tank

The battered view of Stalingrad

12,7 mm anti-aircraft guns

German soldiers go into imprisonment

Italian prisoners of war

October 1942, street fights

Stalingrad, Maxim machine gun

Gathered corpses, Stalingrad January 1943

Fallen soldiers from the 6th Army

Gathered German war vehicles after the battle

Never ending suffering

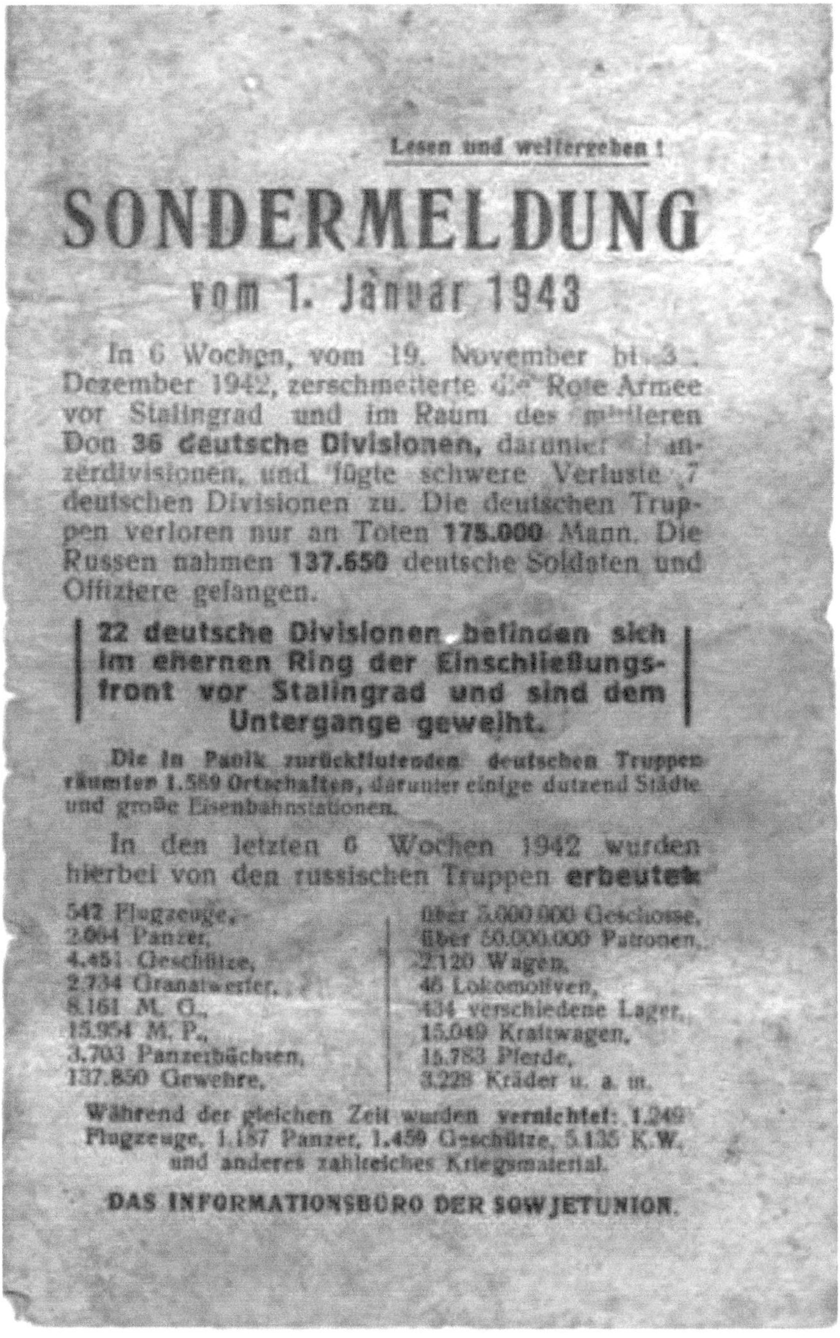

Lesen und weitergeben!

SONDERMELDUNG
vom 1. Januar 1943

In 6 Wochen, vom 19. November bis 3. Dezember 1942, zerschmetterte die Rote Armee vor Stalingrad und im Raum des mittleren Don **36 deutsche Divisionen**, darunter Panzerdivisionen, und fügte schwere Verluste 7 deutschen Divisionen zu. Die deutschen Truppen verloren nur an Toten **175.000** Mann. Die Russen nahmen **137.650** deutsche Soldaten und Offiziere gefangen.

22 deutsche Divisionen befinden sich im ehernen Ring der Einschließungsfront vor Stalingrad und sind dem Untergange geweiht.

Die in Panik zurückflutenden deutschen Truppen räumten 1.569 Ortschaften, darunter einige dutzend Städte und große Eisenbahnstationen.

In den letzten 6 Wochen 1942 wurden hierbei von den russischen Truppen **erbeutet**:

542 Flugzeuge,
2.064 Panzer,
4.451 Geschütze,
2.734 Granatwerfer,
8.161 M. G.,
15.954 M. P.,
3.703 Panzerbüchsen,
137.850 Gewehre,

über 7.000.000 Geschosse,
über 50.000.000 Patronen,
2.120 Wagen,
46 Lokomotiven,
434 verschiedene Lager,
15.049 Kraftwagen,
15.783 Pferde,
3.228 Kräder u. a. m.

Während der gleichen Zeit wurden **vernichtet**: 1.249 Flugzeuge, 1.187 Panzer, 1.459 Geschütze, 5.135 K.W. und anderes zahlreiches Kriegsmaterial.

DAS INFORMATIONSBÜRO DER SOWJETUNION.

Soviet propaganda pamphlet

German soldiers who have surrendered to the Red Army, the second from the right is general Von Seydlitz-Kurzbach

Memorial in honour of the battle

The End of the Air Bridge

It is difficult to ascertain what drove the implementers of the air bridge to continue shedding rations. Other things had long since been abandoned, as survival was now the only thing that mattered. They must not have had any more hope of saving the army. Was it in the spirit of Hitler's decision making to hold the Russians as long as possible, in order to create better conditions on other fronts; was it the will to reduce the suffering of their comrades as much as possible, or was it simply pushing through something they had been doing for two months? The fact is that they were still active in those last few days of the siege. The Soviets soon penetrated the southern part and splintered the German position. It was chaos there. Milch therefore gave orders to drop there only when requested.

- *On 29 January,* Paulus sent another pompous message on Hitler, congratulating him on the 10th anniversary of his seizure of power and ending with 'May our struggle be an example to unborn generations to never give up, no matter how bad things get. Then Germany will triumph. *Heil, mein Führer.*' Fine words, but they could not reverse the calamity and there was no question about 'triumphing'.
- *On 30 January,* 85 more planes flew over Stalingrad and dropped their supplies, especially in the northern part.
- *On 31 January,* Paulus surrendered. Still hearing Hitler's orders,

he did not surrender the army, but only himself. Hitler had promoted him to *Generalfeldmarschall* just the day before. A sign that should be taken as an invitation to end his life himself, because never before had a German field marshal surrendered. Paulus chose to stay alive and at this point finally disobeyed his leader.

Annex: The planes

- Junkers Ju 52
- Heinkel He 111
- Junkers Ju 86
- Focke Wulf FW 200
- Heinkel He 177
- Junkers Ju 290: prototype(2) and
  - first production aircraft(5)
    - Junkers Ju 90

Junkers Ju 52

Around 1910, aircrafts were mainly built of wood and linen, although Anthonie Fokker in particular would make a name for himself with a fuselage of welded steel tubes, covered with linen, but still with wooden wings. At the time, another metal emerged in Germany that proved to be very suitable for aircraft applications. It was an alloy of alu- minium with other metals, mainly copper, and an elaborate heat treatment. It was Hugo Junkers in particular who saw the advantages of this and started building all-metal aircraft in 1916, with the corrugated skin panels in particular being characteristic of his designs. The waves were intended to stiffen the plates so that the skin could also absorb compressive forces. The wave tops were placed in the direction of the airflow as much as possible to reduce the weather resistance it entailed. This culminated in 1930 in the first steps towards the design of the highly successful three-engined Model 52. The Ju 52 has since become a classic, with a status approaching that of the *Douglas Dakota*.

The *Junkers Ju 52* predated the *Dakota,* whose history began in 1933 with the first flight of its predecessor, the DC1. Compared to the *Dakota*, the Ju 52 was nevertheless a little less modern. The *Douglas* had retractable landing gear and a smooth skin. But the *Junkers* was there before it.

Besides the corrugated skin, the so-called 'second wing' stood out as well. It was a non-retractable wing flap whose angle could be adjusted and which reduced the landing speed. The outside of this second wing served as an *aileron*.

Other distinctive aspects of the Ju 52 are the large wing, compared to the fuselage length, and the fact that both wing engines point slightly outwards. Large wing areas, especially in relation to weight, indicate that an aircraft is designed for relatively low speeds, which is also true of the Ju 52. The outward pointing of the engines is intended to keep the aircraft flyable if one of the two wing engines fails.

Before the war, the Ju 52 was used by *Deutsche Lufthansa* as a luxury passenger plane. It accommodated 17 passengers in two single rows at the windows and had gadgets that made it stand out from the competition. For example, there was a folding typewriter attached to a partition that could be used by passengers during the flight. And the on-board marconist, still present at the time, could also send and receive telegrams for passengers.

The *Luftwaffe*, founded in 1935, became a good customer of *Junkers*. The Ju 52 was acquired as a transport aircraft, but also served as a light bomber in the Spanish Civil War and some other campaigns. As a bomber, it was fitted with a retractable gunner's cabin under the fuselage and a fixed one at the top, as shown in the dimensional sketch.

Figures showing production numbers are not always reliable. However, that the Ju 52 was a success and that it was used in large numbers is indisputable. Numbers quoted speak of a total of 4845 aircraft built, and 3500 used by the Luftwaffe.

A notable aspect about every Junkers *aircraft* of the *Luftwaffe* is that Hugo Junkers was a pacifist and critic of the Nazi party. In 1933, his factory was nationalised and a year later he was placed under house arrest. He died before the war began. As a person, he had no hand in the development of the famous *Junkers* warplanes. Although the Ju 52 was used for war purposes, it was designed by him as a civil transport aircraft.

Size sketch and some features

Length: 18.90 m
Span: 29.25 m
Empty weight: 5,720 kg Maximum weight: 10,500 kg Maximum speed: 275 km/h Ceiling: 5900 m
Engines: 3 x *BMW* 132A-3, 541kW

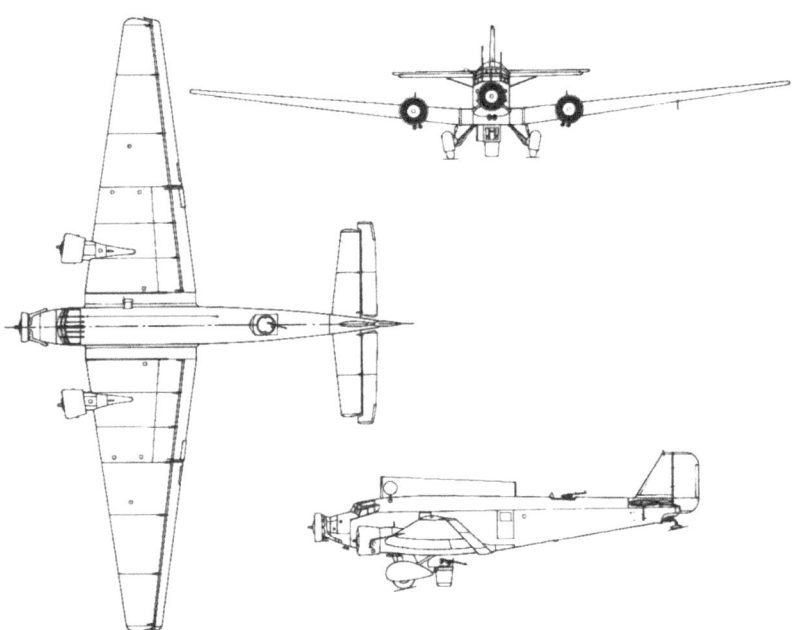

In this photo, you can see some typical characteristics of the Ju 52: the skin of golf plates, the second wing that formed an aileron on the outside, the landing gear and the motors that point to the sides

Heinkel He 111

The history of the *Heinkel He 111* began in the early 1930s, when Germany was starting to build up a military apparatus under the Nazi regime. Unlike Hugo Junkers, Ernst Heinkel was active in designing military aircraft. As an individual, he had already played a role in designing military aircraft in the First World War, but did not own his own factory at that time. The factory had already designed a fast flying aircraft for the civilian market, the *Heinkel He 70*. It was a single-engine aircraft that could seat four passengers. It was the fastest commercial aircraft of its time, characterised by an elliptical gull wing. The elliptical shape probably later inspired the designers of the *Spitfire*.

The brand-new *Luftwaffe* wanted a medium bomber and was impressed by the *Heinkel*'s speed. Based on the He 70 design, the He 111 was built. The aircraft served with the *Lufthansa*, but, according to most experts, was designed with bomber specifications in mind. It was at a time when Germany was not allowed to build a military device. A situation that, as we know, Hitler put an end to in 1935. Until then, the Germans solved it this way. When the curtain fell, the *Heinkel* was converted into a bomber. In the process, its appearance changed in that the *cockpit*, which on the transport aircraft still looked classic as a recognisable 'bulge' behind the nose, now no longer protruded beyond the fuselage lines. In its place came a slightly asymmetrical glass nose, with a reclining gunner's position

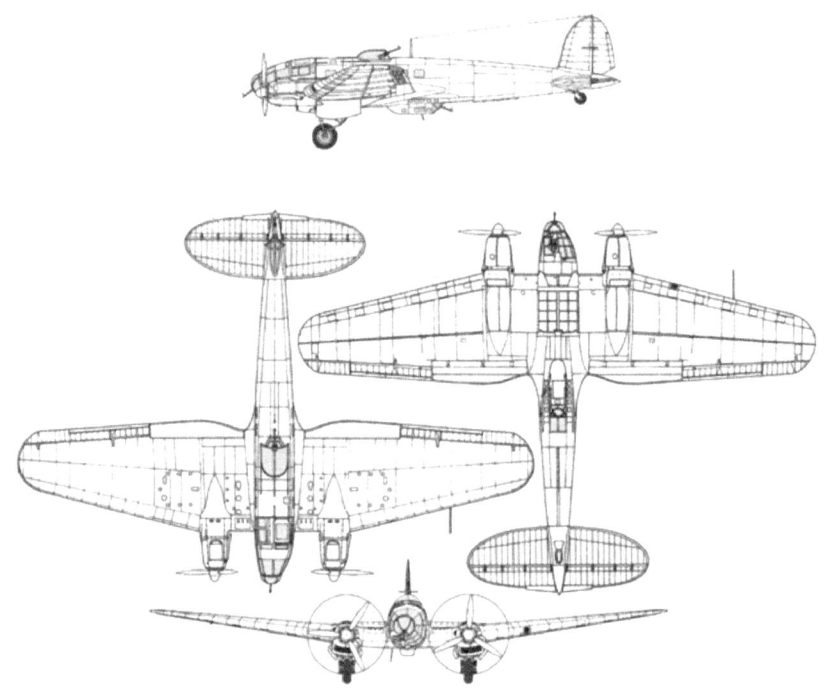

in front and the slightly elevated position for the pilot behind and half next to it. The instrument panel was fixed to the ceiling in a raised position, so that the pilot had an excellent view. The design still provided the familiar tailwheel system, as did almost all aircraft of the time.

The wings, which initially had an elliptical shape like those of the He 70, were later changed to wings with a straight leading and trailing edge.

Along with the *Junkers Ju 52,* the He 111 was the most widely used aircraft for airlift. Earlier, they had been in action in the bombing of Rotterdam.

Size sketch and some features

Heinkel He 111

Length: 16.4 m
Span: 22.6 m
Empty weight: 8,680 kg Maximum weight: 14,000 kg Maximum speed: 440 km/h Ceiling: 7800 m
Engines: 2 × *Jumo* 211F-2 V-12, 1016 kW

The Heinkel He 111 in full flight

Junkers Ju 86

Along with the *Heinkel He 111,* the *Junkers Ju 86* was a response to the, still secret, *Luftwaffe*'s specification for a light bomber. The corrugated skin construction that characterised *Junkers'* previous models was the brainchild of founder Hugo Junkers. Hugo, who emerged as an opponent of the Nazis, was dispossessed, placed under house arrest and had no further involvement in the Ju 86 design. The so-called second wing (see description Ju 52) did remain part of the design.

A special feature of the type was application of diesel motor. Like the *Heinkel,* production was started for both civil and military ver-

On this photo of the Junkers Ju 86, one can clearly spot the second wing

sions. During the Spanish civil war, the *Heinkel* proved more satisfactory at the front, mainly because of the controllability of the engines, but the *Junkers* had its own *niche*. The factory had done a lot of *research* into high-altitude flying. This was exploited by building a version specifically for this purpose. It got a two-man pressurised cabin, special high-altitude engines, extended wings and the gunner's cabins were streamlined. The nose was also radically modified; it became a shorter nose with lots of glass in front. This version reached a ceiling of almost 33,000 ft. Later versions went even further and there was one that reached an altitude of 52,500 ft. These were altitudes that enemy fighters could not reach. This *Junkers* was used for reconnaissance flights.

The Ju 86s used for Stalingrad were cargo versions, not intended for these very high altitudes and mainly used as training aircraft before being sent to the airlift. After the Ju 52 and the He 111, the Ju 86 was the most widely used aircraft in the airlift.

Size sketch and some features

Junkers Ju 86

Length: 16.46 m
Span: 22.5 m
Empty weight: 6,700 kg Maximum weight: 11,530 kg Maximum speed: 300 km/h Ceiling: 6,900 m
Engines: 2 x *Junkers Jumo* 207B-3/V diesel, 447 kW

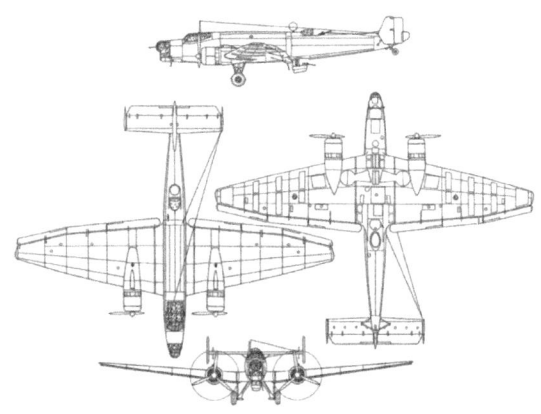

Focke Wulf FW 200

Designed as a long-range transport aircraft, the *Focke Wulf FW 200* deserved a better fate than what came of it through the war. Kurt Tank was *Focke Wulf*'s designer and has a few well-known aircraft to his name, including the FW 190 fighter. His other flagship aircraft was the FW 200.

A version that - unlike several other German transport aircraft - was not intended to be military from the start. It was ordered by Japan, but, due to the outbreak of war, delivery did not materialise, and the type was used by the Germans themselves. It eventually became a formidable naval weapon. Initially as a scout, relaying positions of ships to be attacked by its own vessels, and later in an attack role.

Before Stalingrad, the aircraft was thrown in by the scruff of the neck just to get enough transport capacity. It has not been very fortunate in this role.

Size sketch and some features

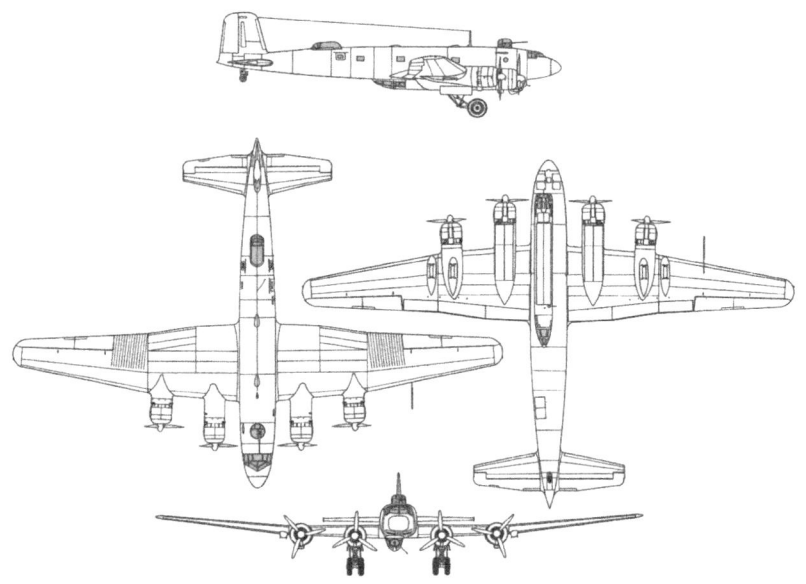

Focke Wulf FW 200

Length: 23.45 m
Span: 32.85 m
Empty weight: 17,005 kg Maximum weight: 24,520 kg Maximum speed: 360 km/h Ceiling: 6,000 m
Engines: *4×BMW/Bramo* 323R-2, 895 kW

The military version of the Focke Wulf FW 200, which visible gun turrets

Heinkel He 177

The most striking thing about the *Heinkel He 177* was that it looked like a twin-engine aircraft, but actually had four engines, two of which drove a single propeller, each in one nacelle. This explains the high power given to the engine in the technical specifications; a paired pair was considered one engine. This unusual arrangement was chosen to reduce drag. Still in the design phase, the *Luftwaffe* demanded that the heavy bomber also be made suitable for the dive-bomber task. In this combination, the *Heinkel* never really worked. The structural requirements for a dive bomber are very high, as the wing is heavily loaded during take-off after the dive.

Partly as a result of efforts to reduce drag - the nacelle was built very tightly around the engines - but also due to other technical reasons, there initially were fire safety problems.

As a result of technical problems, the *Heinkel He 177* was deployed, more or less as a trial, only sparsely in the air bridge to Stalingrad. One of the reasons why its deployment was did not really work was that it could not carry wounded on the way back.

After fixing the problems, the type was later still used fairly successfully in war duties, but did not return to the air bridge.

Size sketch and some features

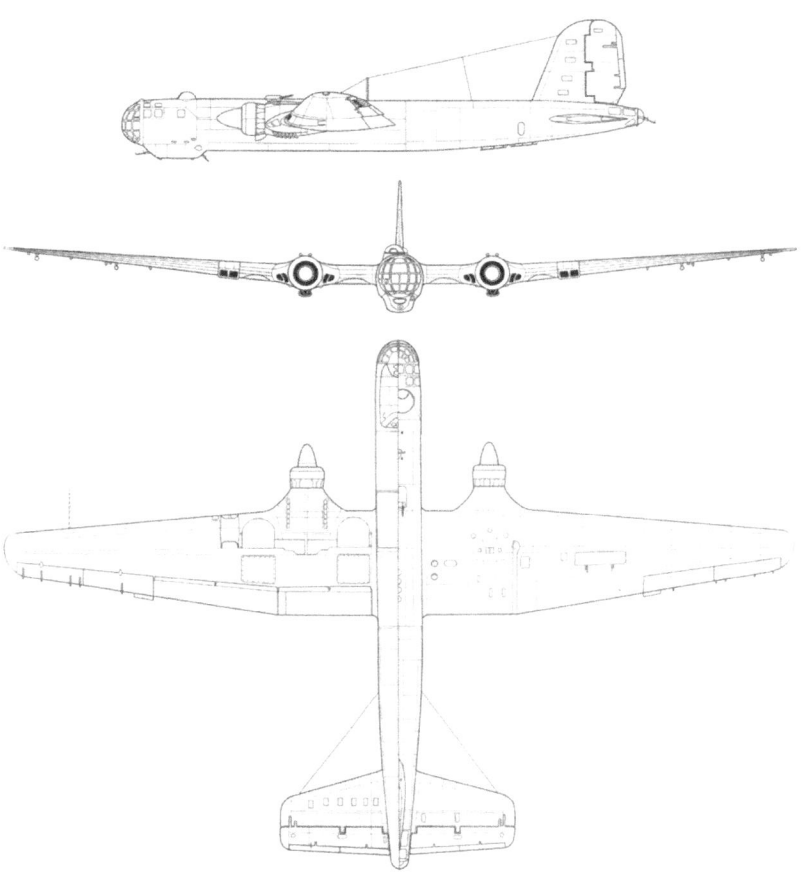

Heinkel He 177

Length: 20.40 m
Span: 31.44 m
Empty weight: 16,800 kg Maximum weight: 31,000 kg Maximum speed: 472 km/h Ceiling: 8,000 m
Engines: *2×Daimler-Benz* DB 610A/B, 2200 kW

The Heinkel He 177. In this picuture is the strange landing gear visible, which consisted out of two legs on either side that were retracted separately

Junkers Ju 90 and Ju 290

The *Junkers* company was commissioned by the *Reichluftfahrtministerium* (RLM) to develop and build a heavy bomber. This was the Ju 89 project. Two prototypes of this were built. Meanwhile, a new wind had changed the RLM's mind in favour of the dive-bomber concept, and the Ju 89 project was stopped. *Deutsche Lufthansa* saw potential in the design as a civil transport aircraft. This became the Ju 90. The Ju 90 possessed many of the features of the Ju 89, and the prototype even still had some parts at the tail with the familiar corrugated plates of the Ju 52, which were changed to smooth plate on later versions. Furthermore, it still possessed the well-known 'second wing' that *Junkers* had applied since the Ju 52.

A need for transport capacity arose at the *Luftwaffe*, and with some minor modifications, the Ju 90 was made into a military transport aircraft. A special feature is the loading door that opened at the bottom and lifted the tail off the ground, see picture.

From the Ju 90, the Ju 290 was developed, with a larger payload and better performance. Notable differences from the Ju 90 were the wing shape, where the 'second wing' had disappeared, and the V-shape of the *stabilo*. Functionality was extended: the Ju 290 was used as a transport aircraft, reconnaissance aircraft, heavy bomber and maritime patrol aircraft. Unlike the Ju 90, the aircraft was equipped with heavy defensive armour.

Neither *Junkers* were deployed in large numbers at the air bridge.

Probably the Ju 290 could have been very successful in it, but it arrived too late to play a significant role.

Size sketch and some features

Junkers Ju 90
Length: 26.5 m
Span: 35.5 m
Empty weight: 19,225 kg Maximum weight: 23,000 kg Maximum speed: 350 km/h Ceiling: 5,750 m
Engines: 4×*BMW* 132H-1, 610 kW

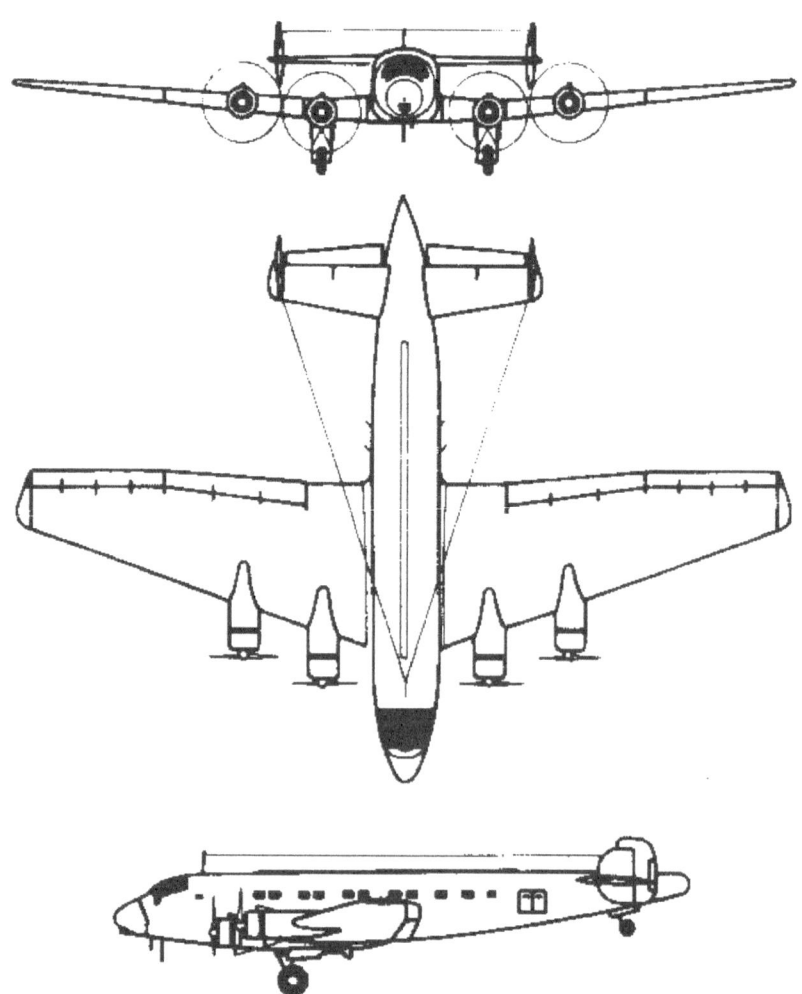

Size sketch and some features

Junkers Ju 290

Length: 28.64 m
Span: 42 m
Empty weight: 33,005 kg Maximum weight: 44,970 kg Maximum speed: 440 km/h Ceiling: 6000 m
Engines: 4×*BMW* 801G/H, 1268 kW

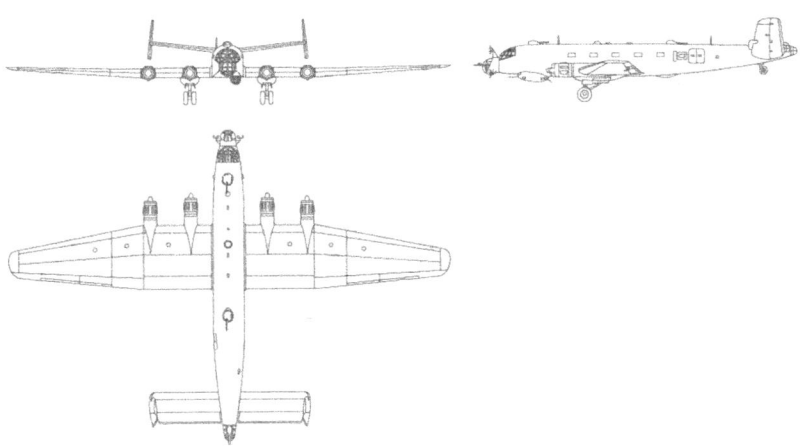

The Junkers Ju 90 in flight. The door could be opened during flight to drop the supplies

A Junkers Ju 290. The armament is clearly visible

Bibliography

Adam, W., *Der schwere Entschluss* (Berlin 1965).

Allaz, C., *The History of Air Cargo and Airmail from the 18th Century.* (Paris 1998)

Beevor, A., *Stalingrad* (London 1998).

Bergström, C., *Stalingrad - The Air Battle: 1942 through January 1943.*
(Hersham 2007)

Carell, P., *Unternehmen Barbarossa. Der Marsch nach Russland.* (Frankfurt am Main 1982)

Carell, P., *Stalingrad. Sieg und Untergang der 6. Armee.* (Frankfurt am Main 1992)

Chaney, O.P., *Zhukov* (New York 1974).

Diedrich, T., *Paulus. Das Trauma von Stalingrad. Eine Biographie* (Pader- born 2009).

Doerr, H., *Der Feldzug nach Stalingrad 1942/1943.* (Friedberg 1954).

Ebener, K., edited by v. Langsdorff, G., *Jagdflieger in Stalingrad.* (1943)

Ebert, J. (hg.), *Stalingrad- eine deutsche Legende.* (Reinbek bei Hamburg 1992)

Erickson, J., *The Road to Stalingrad* (London 1985).

Freese, J., *Schienenstrang nach Stalingrad* (Munich 2003).

Georg, F., *Verrat an der Ostfront.* (Tübingen 2012)

Grams, R., *Die 14. Panzer-Division 1940-1945.* Hrsg. von der Traditions- gemeinschaft, Podzun (Bad Nauheim 1957)

Hayward, J., *Stopped at Stalingrad* (Kansas 1998).

Herhudt von Rohden, H., *Die Luftwaffe ringt um Stalingrad* (Wiesbaden 1950).

Heiber, H. (hg.), *Goebbels Reden 1932-1945.* (Düsseldorf 1972)

Knopp, G., *Entscheidung Stalingrad* (Munich 1992).

Konrad, R, *Kampf um den Kaukasus* ((Munich)

Koschorrek, G.K., *Vergiss die Zeit der Dornen nicht. Ein Soldat der 24. Panzerdivision erlebt die sovjetische Front und den Kampf um Stalingrad* (Würzburg 2004).

Kurowski, F, *Demjansk Der Kessel im Eis* (2001)

Kurowski, F., *Luftbrücke Stalingrad* (Berg am See 1988).

Lower, R., *Luftwaffe Tactical Operations at Stalingrad 19 November 1942 - Fe- bruary 1943. (Air Command and Staff College, report number 87-1595, 1987)*

Magenheimer, H., *Militärstrategie Deutschlands 1940-1945. Führungsent- schlüsse, Hintergründe, Alternative.* (Munich 2002)

Manstein, E. von, *Verlorene Siege.* (Frankfurt am Main 1964).

Maser, W., *Hitlers Mein Kampf. De geschiedenis van het meest omstreden boek. (Soesterberg 2009)*

Meiser, H., *So wurde Stalingrad verraten. Dokumentation und Richtigstel- lung.* (Stegen am Ammersee 2008)

Müller, R-D, (H,G.), *Die Deutsche Wirtschaftspolitik in den bestezten Sowjeti- schen Gebieten 1941-1943. Der Abschlussbericht des Wirtschaftsstabes Ost und die Aufzeichnung eines Angehörigen des Wirtschaftskommandos Kiew* (Boppard am Rhein 1991)

Meyer, H.F., *Blutiges Edelweiss. Die 1. Gebirgs-Division im Zweiten Welt- krieg.* (Berlin 2008)

Panse, E., *Iron Horsemen. The Memoirs of Obergefreiter Ernst Panse, (9/ Pz.Rgt.24) 24 Panzer Division, Stalingrad, 1942-1943.* (Shelf Books no 224
- 2002)

Pätzold, K., *Stalingrad und Kein Zurück, Wahn und Wirklichkeit.* (Leipzig 2002)

Piekalkiewicz, J., *Stalingrad. Anatomie einer Schlacht.* (Munich 1977)

Pierik, P., 'Operatie *Wintergewitter.* De bevrijdingspoging van Stalingrad, december 1942', In; Perry Pierik/Martin Ros, *Tweede Bulletin van de Tweede Wereldoorlog.* (Soesterberg 2000)

Pierik, P., (red.) *Verzet! Swastika onder vuur. Facetten van de weerstand tegen Hitlers 'Festung Europa'.* (Soesterberg 2013)

Pottgiesser, H., *Die Deutsche Reichsbahn im Ostfeldzug 1939-1944.* (Nec- kargemünd 1975)

Reschin, L., *Feldmarschall Friedrich Paulus. Im Kreuzverhör 1943-1953.* (Berlin 2000)

Reuth, R.G., *Goebbels. The Life of Joseph Goebbels. The mephistophelean Genius of Nazi Propaganda.* (London 1993)

Rokossowski, K.K., *Soldatenplicht. Erinnerungen eines Frontbefehlhabers.* (Berlin 1986)

Sapp, F., *Gefangen in Stalingrad 1943-1946.* (Steyr 1992)

Schramm, P.E., *Kriegstagebuch des Oberkommandos der Wehrmacht 1942, Teilband I.* (Munich 1982).

Schukow, *Erinnerungen und Gedanken.* (Stuttgart 1969)

Seewald, B, *Hunger, grösster Feind der Wehrmacht in Stalingrad* (*die Welt* - 2013).

Stahlberg, A., *Die verdammte Pflicht. Erinnerungen 1932 bis 1945.* (Mün- chen 2002)

Taube, G., *Festung Sewastopol* (Berlin/Bonn)

Telpukowski, B.S., *Die Soviet History des Grossen Vaterländischen Krieges 1941-1945.* (Frankfurt am Main 1982)

Tettau, H. von/Versock, K., *Die Geschichte der 24. Infanterie-Division.* (1956)

Traditionsverband 88u. 323 I.D.E.V., Dr Andreas Schwarz, *Woronesh / Don-Stellung 1942/43. Ausgewählte Dokumente* (1977)

Welz, H., *Verratene Grenadiere.* (Berlin 1976)

Werthen, W., *Geschichte der 16. Panzer-Division 1939-1945.* (Bad Nauheim 1958)

Wette, W.,/Ueberschar,G.R., *Stalingrad. Mythos und Wirklichkeit einer Schlacht.* (Frankfurt am Main 1992)

Wijers, H.J., *Der Kampf um Stalingrad. 'Eingeschlossen durch die Rote Ar- mee'. Die Nordriegelstellung.*

Wirta, N., *Die Stalingrader Schlacht.* (Berlin 1948)

Unpublished sources/internet

Tieke, W., *Im Südabschnitt der Ostfront. Die entscheidenden Operationen 1942/43: Crimea, Stalingrad, Caucasia.* (Selbstverlag 1984)

Thyssen, M., *Stalingrad Airlift: The Aircraft.* (Internet article 2007)

Wirtschaftliche Bedeutung Stalingrads.

24. Panzer Division. www.*Lexikon der Wehrmacht.de*

Archive material

BA/MA Freiburg: Kriegstagebuch LII. Armeekorps, Anlage Heft 19 Fern- schreiben an LII. Armeekorps 19.07.1942 18.15 Uhr.

BA/MA Freiburg: Kriegstagebuch Gen.Kdo. LVII.Pz.korps: Komman- deurs Besprechung am 14.07.1942

BA/MA Freiburg, Gen.Kdo. LVII.Pz.korps. Gruppe Kirchner Ia. : 13.Pz.Div., SS-Div.'Wiking', XXXIX.Geb.Armeekorps. Betr.: Erfahrungen über Befesti- gungen Raum Woroschilowgrad zur Weitergabe an die Truppe: Ia nr 1196/42: 19.07.1942

BA/MA Freiburg, Kriegstagebuch nr. 6 Anlage 151-400 Band 2: 18.07.1942- 31.08.1942: 28576/6: Fernschreiben an rom 49 Geb. AK 22.07.1947 (Gruppe Kirchner)

BA/MA Freiburg, Div.Stb.Qu. 16.12.1942: 97. Jäger Division, Divisionsartz: betr: Gesundheitszustand der 97. Jäger Division

BA/MA Freiburg: Gruppe De Angelis 16.01.1943: Betr: Personelle Verluste nach Truppen-krankennachweisen bis 31.Dez.1942

BA/MA Freiburg: Generalkommando LII.A.K. Betr: Ingangsetzung des Berg- baues im Donez-Gebiet 09.07.1942

BA/MA Freiburg F.H.Qu. 1 July 1942: Betr: Wiederaufbau der Kohlenförde- rung im Donezgebiet. (signed by Keitel)

BA/MA Freiburg Nachlass Hermann Breith: Erlebnisse während des 2.Welt- krieges Band 1: Soviet Russia 01.01.1943-11.12.1943

BA/MA Freiburg Korpspionierführer XXXIV.A.K. : Übersicht über die Zerstörungen im Verlauf der Ausweichbewegung auf die Blaue Linie 23.03.1943

BA/MA Freiburg: diary *Von Richthofen BA/MA N 671/9 (1942)*

BA/MA Freiburg: Generalkommando XXXXIX (Geb.) A.K., K.Gef. Stand 01.01.1943: Neujahrsbefehl 1943 File: 35760/2